GW00498757

Traveller in the Glens

Traveller in the Glens

Jack McBride

Appletree Press

First published in 1979 by

Appletree Press Ltd
The Old Potato Station
14 Howard Street South
Belfast BT7 1AP
Tel: +44 (0) 28 9024 3074
Fax: +44 (0) 28 9024 6756
E-mail: reception@appletree.ie
Web Site: www.irelandseye.com

Editor: Jean Brown
Designer: Stuart Wilkinson
Production Manager: Paul McAvoy

Traveller in the Glens

ISBN: 0 86281 937 7

9 8 7 6 5 4 3 2 1

AP3203

Contents

To my dear wife, a Glenswoman born and bred

Foreword

It is gratifying to contribute, no matter in how small a way to a harvest home. That is what *Traveller in the Glens* is, a gathering-in of historical curiosities, tales, customs and ballads, that Jack McBride has gleaned in years of dedicated search through his native glens.

The resumption of regional broadcasting after the war meant a considerable widening of programme output. Improvements in recording technique meant that the voices and opinions of Ulster folk were more readily accessible. Contributors were no longer tied to the studios in Broadcasting House. Producers could wander at will recording men and women in towns, villages and the countryside. But the producer and his team had to find someone who knew the district intimately, someone who could act as guide and counsellor. In my first trip to the Antrim Glens as a BBC producer, back in the forties, I had the great good fortune to meet Jack McBride. On that, and on many subsequent visits I met, through him, such worthies as Maurice Finlay, Mary Stone, Arthur Harvey, Dan McGonnell, James Kelly and Sarah O'Mooney. There was Willie McKillop of Ballybrack who could whistle as sweetly as any blackbird and Mick McAuley with his wealth of memories. Up in windswept Newtowncrommelin Jack and I talked to William McQuitty and were persuaded by his unshakeable confidence in the future of Antrim iron ore.

9

One evening, in a hospitable Waterfoot pub, in the company of Jack and James Delargy the poet, a radio programme, *Country Bard*, was conceived, which, starting off with Glens rhymers such as James Studdert Moore, grew into a series that ran for nine years and broadcast the ballads of almost every country poet, past and present, in the length and breadth of the Province. Jack McBride contributed to those programmes. Indeed, as ballad-maker, story-teller and features writer, he has made a considerable contribution to broadcasting in Northern Ireland.

Many of the stories in this book I recognise with pleasure. The Mystery of the Fuldiew Stone – and its solution – the author has made peculiarly his own. But it would be idle to try to list the topics his questing mind and agile pen have touched upon. Our thanks are due to him and to his publishers for this spicilegium of tales and traditions gathered around one of the most beautiful and historic regions in Ireland.

Sam Hanna Bell

Introduction

The Nine Glens of Antrim have achieved fame by just being themselves – nine beautiful glens! For many centuries most of them were difficult to reach except from the sea or by travelling over rough bridle-paths. There was one coach road from Larne to Glenarm, uphill and down dale, on parts of which passengers had to dismount and utilise shanks' mare while the horses strained to draw the vehicle to the top, and then the anxious driver had to use hand and foot brakes to keep control on the steep descents.

Suddenly – as if at the raising of a giant curtain – the whole Nine Glens became easily accessible! Lanyon's genius overcame the difficulties, unsurmountable as they seemed to other engineers, and a road was constructed that threw open the whole coast from Larne to Cushendall, and linked up with the existing road from there to Ballycastle.

Roadmaking became a popular occupation of County Councils, and soon spread from Ballymena to Glenariff, to Carnlough, to Glenarm and formed a network of communication throughout the county of Antrim. No longer was it necessary for anyone with geese to sell in Belfast to walk them through tar, then sand, then tar again, and so equip them with 'boots' to enable them to cover the long journey to the city without their being footsore as well as weary.

Now they could be accommodated in crates carried by horse-drawn lorries, both the vendor and his geese arriving in tip-top condition!

One man who realised the possibilities in the new access to the fairyland of the Glens was Henry McNeill of Larne, who may justly be regarded as the pioneer of Ulster tourism. He purchased a number of long open cars called charabancs and advertised in the Lancashire, Yorkshire and Cheshire districts by means of leaflets and newspaper ads, even sent couriers to address meetings where the delights of touring the Antrim Coast road were described in detail.

At first tentatively, then in thousands, the tourists flocked to Antrim's coastal resorts, as visitors carried some enthusiastic descriptions of their journey across the sea to Larne, their reception there by Mr 'Knockem-Down' McNeill, their comfortable accommodation in the Main Street and other hotels – and their trips by charabanc round the coast, stopping at Garron Tower for a generous meal, then on to Cushendall, Cushendun, Ballycastle and Portrush, returning via Ballymena to Larne.

I have seen as many as three thousand English visitors arriving at Garron Tower in one day, and very happy they looked, being voluble in their admiration of the beauties and amenities of their excursion.

As regards the people living in the Glens, they are the descendants of both the ancient Irish and their cousins the Hebridean Scots. For many centuries there was constant traffic between the residents on both sides of the Sea of Moyle. At Lammas time there was an annual get-together in Ballycastle which went on for a week, combining both the business and fun-making of a Fair – and, by the same token, a great deal of matchmaking!

Kindness and hospitality are characteristic of Glensfolk, but they are also very keen bargainers, and one would need to be clever to get the better of them. They love music and the traditional airs, and a good musician is always certain of a welcome at a ceilidh or any celebration.

Country poets are treated with the respect once accorded to the bards, and their verses are quoted by young and old as words of wisdom or wit. Some of the major poets (John Hewitt for example) have derived inspiration from the Glens, and poets like Moira O'Neill have written verses in the local dialect.

It was customary in the old days to find one of the ballad-makers attending a regatta, a horse-race or an election meeting, and later to find him distributing or singing a ballad descriptive of the event.

Like their bardic predecessors they could be quite satiric if they felt that such an approach was deserved, and many a wrongdoer 'cleared the country' rather than be subjected to the irony and invective of the local 'poet'.

Today, with all the modern incitements to a 'fast' life the people of the Glens remain honest, hard-working and masters – not servants – of time, ready to share a joke, a meal, a bottle – but never a sweetheart!

Now let us embark upon our adventure – our visit to the Nine Glens. Like the Glens themselves, we must adapt to the surroundings, going slowly when we savour some enchanting view, then stopping for a chat with, or about, some local character.

We may paint in the background by glimpses of history, or

by a local poet's impression of a particular event, but let us make certain to keep our minds receptive to the atmosphere of a district that inspired Thackeray to wax lyrical about it, or John Masefield, whose wife was one of the Crommelins, a local family, to refer to:

> That curlew-calling time in Irish dusk
> When life becomes more splendid than its husk.

Come on then, let's go!

1

The Southern Glens

Glenariff is easily the best known of Antrim's Nine Glens, visited by thousands of people from all over the world. Strangely, though, there are many interesting, beautiful and historic places between the Red Arch and the Garron Head almost invariably overlooked by these visitors, so we'll have a glance at some of them.

Red Bay Castle

Let us commence our tour at Red Bay Castle, the ruins of which are a monument to our troublous early history. At one time this was the principal dwelling-place of the McDonnells of the Glynnes (Glens), 'Lords of the Isles' as they called themselves, and many were the sieges the strongly-fortified castle withstood, such as when (in 1565), Shane O'Neill, then at the height of his power, attacked and captured it on his way to encounter Sorley Boy McDonnell at Glentaisi. In the subsequent battle O'Neill was victor, but the McDonnells avenged their defeat when they decapitated O'Neill at Cushendun a couple of years later.

In 1585 the restored castle figured in another siege, this time unsuccessful, and had peace then until 1597, in which year the McDonnell chieftains made Glenarm and Dunluce their main strongholds, abandoning Red Bawn (Bay) to moulder slowly to decay.

Underneath its crumbling walls the red sandstone has been tunnelled into caves, one of which led under the present coast road Red Arch, and had its exit on the beach. (This opening has now been closed to keep cattle from straying into the cave.)

When the castle was occupied, these caves were useful for the storage of food and weapons, and for living accommodation when the retainers of the clan gathered there for safety during the progress of a feud. Again, if the castle was surrounded by enemies, these exits were useful for sallying forth and surprising the invader!

Crooksnavick (or Crookanavick), 'The Hill of Creeping', was when trying to climb this slope and take the defenders by surprise.

Leaving the historic ruin behind us, and travelling along the old road constructed in the middle of the last century by order of Francis Turnley, we next come to the spot where stood the old RC church, the ground for which was obtained from the above-mentioned Turnley.

Not far away is Court McMartin, or Castle Hill, where the Mandevilles or de Mandevilles are said to have had one of their castles. The local gaol and gallows were later erected on the site, and many stories are current about trials and executions held there.

The Feis

The Glens Feis, or Feis na nGleann, was founded in 1904 and since then it has been held annually in one or another of the Nine Glens. In 1944 it was decided that for the following years the venue should be Glenariff, scene of the first feis.

Feis day, Thursday, June 30th 1904 was the occasion of the

biggest assembly of Glensfolk ever know, augmented, too, by many people from all over Ireland.

Most of those prominent on that day, including Sir Horace Plunkett (who delivered the feis oration), Francis J. Biggar, Miss Barbara McDonnell, John Clarke ('Benmore'), Sir Hugh Smiley, Ronald McNeill (later Lord Cushendun), Sir Daniel Dixon, Roger Casement, Andy Dooey and Dr Douglas Hyde, people whose interest in the feis never flagged, have all passed away, but the tradition is ably carried on by a local committee.

The scene as the crowds formed up in procession near Cushendall, then marched from that to Waterfoot, was one that has never left the memory of anyone privileged to have witnessed it. Bands, some in costume, led various contingents, and choirs added their voices to the general harmony.

Out in Red Bay, gaily decorated, lay the yachts of Sir Hugh Smiley and Mr Thos. Jack; all the houses were newly whitewashed and bore many coloured streamers, and everyone felt that the day was to be a success. It was, as witnessed by the fact that the feis has endured since 1904.

Glenariff was, some ninety years ago or so, the centre of a flourishing iron-ore industry, but that period of the Glen's history deserves an article to itself, so we may only take a glance in passing at the White Arch, across which passed so many thousands of tons of ore on their way to the holds of the ships that conveyed them to the furnaces of Cumberland.

The Ardclinis Crosier

Round the quaintly-named Dog's Nose Point, we see that the ancient graveyard and what remains of the monastery of Ardclinis, where it is said a stone once stood which had a marvellous power: no matter how weary the traveller, he had but to sit on that stone for a few minutes, and arise refreshed!

An interesting legend is attached to Ardclinis Monastery. According to this, St Kieran, whose community at Layde (across Red Bay) was threatened with starvation, came to the Abbot and asked his prayers, saying that their corn would not be ready for at least another month. 'A month? echoed the Abbot, 'See! Your corn is already ripe!' And when St Kieran looked over across the Bay – there stood the field of corn, turned to a beautiful golden yellow, all ready for the reapers.

It was at Ardclinis, too, that a crosier, called 'Bachil McKenna', was for many years in use by local people as a venerated object utilised in the taking of oaths or in the detection of false statements. Tradition has it that if anyone stole anything from his neighbour, was accused, denied his guilt, and was brought to swear upon the crosier, then if he were really guilty the stolen goods would appear at his feet to compound his perjury.

This crosier was taken by a man called Galvin to his home near Glenarm where he used it to hold harness in his stable until someone made him aware of its antiquity and value. Thereafter it occupied an honoured place in his household, and is at present in the possession of the Magill family of the Cairncastle district. St MacNissius of Connor is said to be buried in Ardclinis.

Leaving Ardclinis, we come to a wild-looking part of the road, fringed by tall limestone cliffs, whose extra whiteness seems to indicate that they have been the scene of quarrying operations. Older residents remember that about forty years ago the Falavee quarries and pier were flourishing, many cargoes of limestone being shipped to Glasgow and other ports, until one wild night the sea carried off the end of the pier, badly damaged the remainder, and created such havoc that it was decided by the directors of the company to concentrate all their business at Carnlough.

The loads of 'quarry-redd' are mute tokens of a once-flourishing industry, and who knows what secrets still lie hidden in the caves that tunnel through the cliffs? During the few years the quarrying operations lasted, a number of skeletons and skulls were found in rock crevices, a reminder – so local residents aver – of the days when the only pass or thoroughfare around the coast was over these rocks.

It seems that a gang of robbers made the nearby village of Galbolly their headquarters, and frequently waylaid travellers. One more circumstantial tale than the rest refers to a certain Jaspar Fairey, who accumulated riches in the form of precious stones and a bag of gold. When in Larne, Jaspar must have unwisely allowed somebody to see his store, somebody in league with the Galbolly gang, for the news of his coming arrived a couple of days before he was seen making his way over Foran Path and up Deragh Pass on what was to prove his last journey. What happened we can only guess, but the finding of a man's skull with the track of an axe in it during operations at Falavee quarry seems to hint at one solution of the riddle. To get back to the local story: when Jaspar Fairey did not arrive at his native place (somewhere near Coleraine) his friends instituted inquiries, and when the Galbollians thought a search might be made they hid the jewels, retaining only the gold, which they divided among the gang. Nobody was brought to justice, but it is likely that some crevice at Falavee holds a fortune in jewels awaiting an owner!

Galbolly's Booley

Galbolly, the village mentioned above, is a peaceful law-abiding place these days, but for all that it has in winter a queer, eerie appearance – perhaps an echo of its lawless days, and it is a strange fact that for three months of the year, December, January and February, not a direct ray of sunshine ever shines into its houses or over its fields!

It was long the custom in mountainous districts for the people to put in their crops in the lowland fields, then migrate to the mountainy upper-lands, where they stayed during the summer, grazing their cattle and sheep.

The Galbolly folk followed this custom for centuries, and today, on the mountains overlooking this 'Hidden Village', the remains of the 'booley', or clachan of beehive-shaped huts, may clearly be traced. In *Here's Ireland* by Harold Speakman (Robt. McBride & Co., New York, 1931) a most interesting account of an American's tour through Ireland with a donkey, the following passage occurs relative to 'booleys': 'Here is the surprising testimony of Sir Wm. Wilde, written in 1835: "There are several village in Achill, particularly those of Keene and Keele, where the huts of the inhabitants are all circular or oval, and built for the most part of round, water-washed stones, collected from the beach, and arranged without lime or any other cement, exactly as we have reason to believe that the habitations of the ancient Firbolgs were constructed.

"During the spring the population of several of the villages we allude to in Achill close their winter dwellings, tie their infant children on their backs, carry with them their loys (narrow spades) and some corn and potatoes, with a few pots and cooking utensils, drive their cattle before them, and emigrate to the hills, where they find fresh pasture for their flocks, and there they build rude huts or summer houses of sod and wattle called booleys and then cultivate and sow with corn a few fertile spots in the neighbouring valleys. They thus remain for about two months of the spring and early summer till the corn is sown. Then, their stock of provisions being exhausted and the pasture consumed by the cattle, they return to the shore and eke out a miserable and precarious existence by fishing, etc. No further care is ever taken of the crops".'

There we have a picture of the booley system, and the remains on Galbolly Top show that the custom existed there down to fairly recent times.

Cushendall

Cushendall, referred to by an old writer as a 'neat village', remains a neat village to this day, though it has begun to throw out suburbs in a rather unplanned manner. It is built down into a little glen (the two sloping banks of the River Dall) and as we enter it we observe, at the junction of Shore Street and Mill Street, a queer-looking battlemented building erected by Turnley in 1801 as a sort of guardhouse. Thackeray mentions Cushendall in his *Irish Sketch Book*, having stayed for some days in the inn that once stood where Stone's shop is now.

The beauty of Cushendall and Cushendun have inspired both poet and painter, and the late J. Humbert Craig made his home at Rockport Cushendun, many of the lovely spots around there being the subject of some of his best work.

Everyone knows Thomas Moore's *Silent, O Moyle*, a poem inspired by the legendary Children of Lir, who were condemned to roam the Sea of Moyle under the guise of swans, their 3,000-

year sentence ending only when the first Christian bell was heard ringing out over the 'dark stormy waters'.

There is a local belief that the place whence the children were first despatched on their long banishment was a little 'port' (or small-boat harbour) just north of Legge Green, and it was to here they returned to die when the ordeal was over.

Cushendall was at one time the site of a flourishing munition factory, at Tievebulliagh! Now, don't rush off to write to your MP asking why this local industry was allowed to die out! Cushendall must have been very busy then – in the Stone Age – supplying axe-heads, arrow-heads and the like, the plentiful quantity of flints in the district providing an inexhaustible supply of raw material for manufacturing them.

The antiquary has here a rich field, and many fine specimens of prehistoric workmanship have been found during excavations or ordinary farming operations.

In the old days it was a common enough thing for the farmers, stock-breeders and fishermen of the Glens to sail across to the markets of West Scotland with their produce, bringing back changes of seed potatoes, cattle and the small hardy breed of Highland horse or pony. It was found that these ponies and their progeny, when crossed with locally-bred animals, produced a pony of a superior type. Over a century ago the McAuleys of Glenville laid the foundation of the type with some thoroughbred sires, including an Arab, and nearly all the locally-bred sires were first or second crosses of this stock.

Three sires, 'Low Ben', 'Tom-Tit' and 'Trillion', all thoroughbred, were later supplied by the McDonnell and Pilkington families, 'Low Ben' in particular being noteworthy, the best of the mares tracing their breeding to him.

Unfortunately, some breeder tried introducing the Clydesdale type and then, finding the experiment unsuccessful, thought to rectify matters by crossing with the Welsh cob or Irish draught horse, but the only result was to almost eliminate the 'Cushendall Pony' as a distinct type.

Prior to the 1914–18 conflict a commission was appointed to inspect all breeds of ponies in the British Isles with a view to finding the type most likely to make a good polo pony when crossed with a suitable thoroughbred.

This commission reported that the 'Cushendall' type bred in the Glens of Antrim was the animal most suited for the purpose, but further action in the matter was prevented when war broke out.

Nowadays only a few examples of the once-famous pony remain, and in a few years even these must go, which is a pity for the 'Cushendall' was one of the best things of its size in horseflesh! It was a tough, wiry, fiery and almost tireless. It was as good a forager as a mountain goat, and almost as sure-footed, was in no way hard to feed, yet when well groomed it showed the beauty of its Arab ancestry.

It could draw a trap at a spanking pace on a Sunday or haul a plough with its team-mate on Monday, and was so docile that it was in great demand as a children's mount as it developed a dog-like devotion to its little master or mistress.

Let us hope some lover of a grand little animal may yet take steps to prevent its extinction. It is quite possible for a modern farmer to admire both a good tractor and a good horse!

Overlooking Cushendun is Glenville 'Castle', a building which was once the ancestral home of the McAuley family to which belonged John Boyd McAuley, believed by many people to be the author of the famous *Letters of Junius*. There is a queer inscription above the gateway of this house: 'Dulce Periculum, Boots and Spurs'.

The cone-shaped hill above High Street, called Tiveragh, is reputed to be haunted by fairies, and some years ago a local resident, Mr McCambridge, broadcast an account of his encounter with some of the 'wee people' whom he disturbed during their hurling game! Odd though this story sounded, it is paralleled by another experience related to the writer by a native of the district who died, aged over 80, some years ago:

'I was about six at the time and one day my mother sent me out to gather a wheen o' twigs to put in under the griddle to quicken the fire. There was a scroggery o' hazels on the sides o' Tiveragh at that time and I was busy gatherin' away when I heard a fisslin' beside me. I looked up an' there – with his back to me – was what I took to be a wee lad about my own height, from the village Cushendall. Now, at times when I had been alone in Cushendall, some of the young lads had called things at me, wantin' to fight an' so on, an' I thought here was a chance to get my own back. I dropped the sticks an' made for him, but the minute he heard the feet he took at it, runnin' for lives a side roun' the hill!

'I was souple as a hare myself, an' very soon was overhaulin' him but – I mind it yet! – just as I went to lay my hand on his shoulder he turned round, an' there was the face of an oul', oul' man girnin' at me!

'You may be sure I took to the baters on the other road an' niver stopped till I got home.

'The minute I got in, an' me all scared-lookin', my mother noticed it, an' saw I hadn't the sticks.

"What ails ye, Achray?" says she, so I told her.

"That wasn't a wean from the town," says she. An' for all that day an' the next she didn't let me even go out over the threshold of our dure!'

Cushendall has changed its name as often as a Hollywood star! In her grant of it to Henry Knollys, Comptroller of the Royal Household in 1574, Queen Elizabeth refers to it as 'Bournay Dall', though its name in the original Gaelic was 'Cosabhan' Dalla'. Sorley Boy McDonnell owned it for a while, then the Hollow Sword Blade Company of London acquired it and sold it to a Dr Richardson who changed its name to Newtownglens.

Francis Turnley bought it from Richardson and with good judgement restored its name to something like its original appellation, and Cushendall it has remained ever since.

The history of the Turnley family since its arrival in the district is a record of pioneering in the opening up and advancement of the stretch of coast from Drumnasole to Cushendall.

Francis Turnley, who hailed from England, was a younger son who was sent out East in the days when money could be acquired there. He appears to have been gifted with the necessary acquisitive sense as he landed home in five years with a nice little nest-egg: £80,000!

Being a little feudal-minded (his will was set aside later on because his relatives claimed he wasn't sane), he had a square tower constructed which he called the Curfew Tower, the tenant of which had to ring the curfew bell at certain times each day, faithful performance entitling him to occupy the Curfew Tower rent free.

The first custodian of this stronghold was Dan McBride, an ex-army man. The bell was rung at 8 am, 1, 6 and 9 pm and visitors sometimes wondered what the tintinabulation meant (the bell used had by no means the majesty or melody of Big Ben!).

Francis Turnley was also responsible for the construction of the first good road leading from Carnlough through what is now Garron Tower demesne, around the coast via Waterfoot to Cushendall.

The making of the Larne–Cushendall coast road at a later date made parts of this original road obsolete, but the stretches still in use pass through some lovely countryside, notably from Carnlough to Drumnasole, from thence to Ballyvilligan and from the 'Cut Rock' to the 'White Lady'.

On one side is the tree-clad slope, rising to the overhanging black rock, on the other is a view of the sea with the Mull of Cantyre and other parts of the Scottish Coast looming in the distance.

Drumnasole house is a pleasant, roomy residence, set among trees about half a mile from the coast road. Near it, beside the old road that formerly carried all the round-coast traffic, is the old schoolhouse.

A little further on is a low wall of stones blocking the road, but a stile leads over this and on the other side is Tubberdoney which was at one time a highly esteemed 'Holy' (or curative) well, its water being reputed to be most efficacious in the treatment of eye troubles.

The 'Goat's Parlour'

A path starts from near the well and following it (in spring passing fields of glorious daffodils, for which Drumnasole is famed), we come to the 'Goat's Parlour', beyond which is the waterfall.

'Goat's Parlour' is a quaint name for an arched almost-cavern, which was much frequented by these animals in the days when large numbers of them roamed half-wild over the countryside.

There are few goats left about Drumnasole now, and no wild ones, the nearest wild specimens being those frequenting the rocks above Falavee, Ardclinis, but the view of the waterfall from the 'parlour' is memorable. I remember visiting the fall at the same time as a Manchurian who was staying in the vicinity during a break in his studies at Queen's University. When he and his friend first sighted it he tried to convey his feelings in English – and his English was good – but found this inadequate, and finished up in voluble, if to me incomprehensible – Chinese!

His usual impassivity deserted him and by most impressive gestures he conveyed his delight at the beauty of the scene.

The foam-flecked water flows to the edge of the cliff, then is hurled down the rockside to end its turbulent career in the dark depths of the pool below, where (bearing froth 'like an old-time pint', as one regretful oul' drouth described it!) it settles itself into a deceptive stillness, later resuming its journey to the sea as a little singing trill that sounds as peaceful as a mother crooning a lullaby.

The sides of the fall are clothed in verdure, ferns, foxgloves, primrose plants and the leaves of the hazel forming a green background for whatever flowers are in season. No better spot could be found for the poet or those other daydreamers known as honeymooners!

'The Lettered Rock'

Near Garronpoint we notice a flat-fronted rock alongside the road. Called locally 'The Lettered Rock' it is well worth seeing. It bears the following inscription:

Francis Anne Vane
Marchioness of Londonderry
Being Connected With this Province
By the Double Ties of Birth and
Marriage
AND
Being Desirous To Hand Down To
Posterity
AN IMPERISHABLE MEMORIAL
OF IRELAND'S AFFLICTION
IN THE YEAR 1846–47
Unparalleled In The Annals of
Human Suffering
HATH ENGRAVED THIS STONE.
Fair Tablet, fashioned by the Almighty's Hand
To guard these confines of the sea and land:
No longer shall thou meet the stranger's sight
A polished surface of unmeaning white,
But bid him ponder on the days of yore;
When Plague and Famine stalked along the shore
And pale Hibernia veiled her drooping head –

Somebody chipped away the rest of the writing many years ago, but there is enough in the extract given to remind us of that terrible time in our history.

Garron Tower and District

Let us use our magic carpet to convey us to the slopes of Garron, that headland visible from Torr Head, from Ballygally, or from the Mull of Cantyre (nearest point in Scotland). Here we have some of the most rugged scenery of the Antrim Coast, mingled with spots like Garron Tower where the wealth of greenery and flora equals that of the mildest spots on the coasts of Cornwall or Cork.

The first point of interest after passing Galbolly is Clochastookan, or 'The Stone of the Stump' (well-named as it is shaped like the stump of a tree). This stone was mentioned by the historian Keating as one of the points – the other being Mizen Head – whence the length of Ireland was measured in olden times.

A few hundred yards farther on is the 'White Lady' (sometimes erroneously confused with Clochastookan), a large limestone rock which from some angles resembles the figure of a woman in early Victorian dress and carrying a basket over one arm.

In Hall's *Ireland*, published in the early 1800s, there is a drawing of this stone and when compared with the White Lady of today it can be seen that she has altered but little in contour since then, though she is now farther from the sea, due to the construction of the coast road between her and the water.

A little way round the first bend in the road was Garronpoint School which, until a few years ago, carried an inscription recording the fact that it was built in 1847 by Frances Anne Vane, then Marchioness of Londonderry. By the way, an even older school building was that at Kilmore, Glenariff, erected in 1835 and according to modern standards capable of accommodating about 25 pupils. It had upwards of 50 on the rolls! It has recently been converted to a private dwelling.

The Great Famine

The famine of 1845–47 was, we know, due to the failure of the Irish potato crop, a crop upon which the people had come to rely more and more as their staple article of food.

When blight struck the crop it also signed the death warrants of over a million people, those who survived the undernourishment being so weakened that they fell easy victims to famine's jackals, typhus, dysentery and typhoid.

'Indescribable scenes were witnessed all over the land, men, women and children died along the roadsides or in the fields where they were trying to support life by eating grass or roots. Babies died because their mothers were unable to nourish them, and in many cases the only survivors of whole families were an old grandfather or grandmother, whose enforced fast did not seem to affect them as it did the more active.'

The district from Glenarm to Cushendall did not suffer nearly so severely as other places owing to the common-sense way in which Lord Antrim, Lady Londonderry and Francis Turnley acted in the emergency.

Turnley put gangs of men to work at making roads, thus opening up hitherto almost inaccessible stretches of the Antrim countryside, and giving farmers a better chance of marketing their produce in future years. These men were recruited from the poorest class, and if their payment was small, at any rate it helped them to tide over the Famine period.

The memory of that terrible time is preserved not only on the 'Lettered Rock', but also in local tradition. When anyone travelling over the mountains complains that he suddenly became very hungry on the way, someone is sure to remark, 'Ye be to hev walked over a patch o' hungry grass' – 'hungry grass' being what grew after the herbage was devoured by famine victims.

Not many people who cross over the Glenariff River (the 'Acre') now that its course was once through the other side of the Glen, about half-way along Ligatallen, at which point it entered the bay.

One of the relief schemes during the famine was the altering of the river's course, the object in this alteration being the prevention of the flooding which frequently occurred after heavy rains. That this plan was not entirely successful is proved by the periodical inundations which take toll of the crops in the lower reaches, but as a 'relief' scheme it certainly saved many people from starvation.

The two foremen on the job were imported, their names being Whelan and Smith, and their harsh treatment of the workers is remembered in stories told of that time. It is said that a favourite call of these well-fed bullies was: 'Move along, you Irish — ! Two men could drag the 'ole – passel of you to Cawrick!' (Carrickfergus, the jail at that time).

Building Garron Tower

As already mentioned, in the first of the Famine years Lady Londonderry started the building and laying-out of the grounds of the mansion which she named 'Garron Tower', and thus gave much-needed employment to the local people.

Payment was small (tenpence a day for labourers, and a shilling for tradesmen!) but she supplemented this with meal and other foodstuffs, so that the number of workmen grew and the large battlemented edifice was erected in record time. The arrangement of the grounds she personally superintended.

Most of the interior of the mansion was, sad to say, destroyed by fire many years ago. Built on a commanding site near the summit of Garron Head, it had hundreds of rooms including a beautifully panelled ballroom, dining room and library, whose carvings must have been executed by a man with the soul of an artist. Furnished in the very best style of the period, it contained also many splendid paintings such as that of the Duchess of Buckingham (valued at £10,000).

When completed, Lady Londonderry gave many parties and balls there, but her greatest pleasure was in travelling about her domain in a carriage drawn by a pair of black Russian ponies.

'Her Ladyship's Path', a steep track leading up to the mountain top was a favourite route, and her old coachman, the late 'Jamie' Black (died about 1930, aged 104) told how she used to leave the carriage at the rock-heads, seat herself on the heather and spend hours in admiration of the magnificent view from their vantage point, or in writing poems descriptive of it. (Were these ever published, I wonder?)

The above-mentioned Jamie Black was a wonderful old man when the writer first met him. Although partly crippled, he was always cheerful, always ready for a chat, and attributed his longevity to the fact that he never let a day pass without drinking a glass of sea water!

Her Ladyship had a spaniel of which she was very fond and when it died of old age, she caused a headstone to be erected over its burial-place, with the following inscription:

Here Urisk lies, and let the truth be told,
This faithful dog was blind, infirm and old;
Deaf though he was, his mistress's voice he knew,
Blind though he was, his step to her was true.
So strong a spirit by affection fed,
Endured till Urisk's vital spirit fled.
Stoop grandeur from thy lofty throne, Ye Sons of Pride
To whom no want is known, nor wish denied,
A moment pause, then blush, if blush ye can,
To find in dogs more virtue than in man;
And spare, midst all your luxury and pelf,
One thought for others out of ten for self.

Her Ladyship fitted out the embrasures in the walls with cannon said to have seen service in the Crimea, and it was her whim that a brass cannon should be kept ready to return her salute when her yacht came to anchor off Garron.

She had a fine rosery constructed, and until recently this contained some of the finest examples of the queen of flowers to be found anywhere.

The garden, too, was very well tended, the head gardener, the late Gideon McGalliard, having learnt his job in the gardens and conservatories of the Duke of Bedford.

In the garden was a eucalyptus tree, believed to be the largest in Europe, and the water pumped up to Garron Tower from the water-mill at Foran comes from the smallest river in Ireland. The Shannon is 250 miles long, the Foran 250 feet!

Garron Tower is now a boys' secondary school, St MacNissi's College, which is fast gaining a name as one of the most progressive and successful of its kind in Ulster.

The Fort of Dunmaul

Even as far back as pre-Christian times and up to the 15th century, the Garron district was of importance as a recognised meeting-place for Antrim's petty chieftains when paying tribute to their overlord. Dunmaul Fort, on the top of Garron Head, was where this annual hosting took place and also where beacon fires were lighted to summon the Antrim men's Scottish friends in time of need.

At the foot of this headland are several caves. One of them penetrates nearly a hundred feet, but was deeper until 50-odd years ago, when a fall of rock blocked it almost half way. These caves were all at one time used by smugglers whose activities were little hindered by a coastguard station on top of the next headland (to seaward of the 'Cut Rock').

Some tales are current of battles between the Revenue men (or coastguards) and the duty-dodgers, but it appears that the only times the smugglers were interfered with were when they carried defiance too far, and tried contraband-running in daylight! Later, when we reach Ringfad, we can hear the story of what happened to the last big cargo of dutiable goods.

About half a mile from The Tower on 'Turnley's Branch" is a graveyard, Nappan, where the Turnleys and Higginsons are buried. (The elder Mrs Turnley was a sister of the famous poetess Moira O'Neill, née Higginson, whose son John Turnley served as MP for the district.) This graveyard is reputed to have been used as such for the past 1,000 years, though no mention of it can be found in old records.

'Queen Anne'

Many of the older visitors to the Garron district will remember

Miss Anne McNeill, 'Queen Anne', who was postmistress there
until her death some fifty years ago.

Born in Waterfoot, she was reared on Nappan mountain,
where her father was shepherd and gamekeeper, and she very
early displayed an aptitude for learning which she was to retain
during her lifetime.

After her appointment it became an accepted thing for many
Antrim Coast visitors to include a visit to 'Queen Anne's' post
office in their tour, for there one could be sure of a fresh item of
news, a kindly welcome and the stimulation of the hearty, pealing
laughter for which she was renowned.

In youthful days she acquired the sobriquet 'Queen Anne' as
a tribute to her deportment. She was a fine figure of a woman,
almost six feet tall and 'Point' people recall her appearance at a
dance in Garron Tower where she sailed majestically into the
ballroom attired in a costume which made her look as regal as
anything her famous namesake can have worn. Her sense of
humour was shown by the fact that her dress (of dark rich velvet)
had a long train which was borne by a little lad in page's dress!

As James Kelly, a local versifier, described it:

> The stately 'Queen' whose flowing train
> A page-boy carried high,
> While filmy lace that veiled her face
> Caught many a wondering eye.

Miss Anne kept a few goats which sometimes in their wanderings
strayed out of the woods (where they were allowed undisturbed)
on to the lawns and gardens. Repeated warnings to the owners of
the Garron goat population had no effect – as one old lady

remarked plaintively: 'Dae they think the bits o' goats can read they notices' – so Anne among others received a personal letter telling her that proceedings would be instituted forthwith if the animals were not 'langled', or otherwise kept under some measure of control.

Anne's reaction to this were the following lines (which she composed the same day she received the letter) written boldly in her beautiful calligraphy, and pinned up for all to see:

> There is a little creature that through the woodland dotes,
> But men of fame have changed her name
> She's now 'that bl––y goat'!
> When Londonderry's spaniel died she gave it lasting fame
> By putting up a tombstone and recording Urisk's name;
> But if our goat should chance to stray,
> While on the lawn it grazes,
> The men who rule the Tower today
> Would blow poor Bess to blazes!
> So we must keep our goat at home
> To tie and starve in crew [goathouse].
> Forbidden anywhere to graze,
> What else can poor Bess do?
> Before we'd let that fate befall,
> We'd use the pot and pan,
> And monument she'd have enough,
> She'd rest then with 'Queen Anne'.

Anne's brother, 'Wee Henry', who was a carpenter, was given a job renovating the glass and frames on the upper parts of the Garron Tower greenhouses. While thus engaged, one of the directors of the firm happened to be visiting the garden, and went into the greenhouse on whose roof Henry chanced to be working.

'Well, Henry, how are you getting along?' he asked, looking up.

'Fine, Mr —, fine!' said Wee Henry, who had a slow, pedantic way of speaking, 'as you perceive, this is a job that calls for the exercise of great circumspection. Had it have been given to a man of less experience than I — ' and at that moment, missing his footing, he fell across the frames and panes he had just repaired, and landed along with the wreckage at the other man's feet!

On another occasion Anne had some unexpected visitors in the shape of a couple of HQ Post Office officials.

The door to her kitchen opened off the 'business' part of the house, and while her visitors were engaged in their check-up she returned to finish her interrupted dinner, which consisted mainly of 'dab at the stool' (potatoes and salt).

Wee Henry had almost finished his, but this is some of what the visitors were – and were not – meant to hear:

'Oh, Henry, dear, so you have almost finished luncheon?'

'Eh?'

'I said, Henry, my dear, you almost finished your repast. Was everything to your pleasement?'

(One can picture the silent pantomime, then Henry must have grasped the situation.)

'Oh yes, Anne, dear. Everything was most appetising except that the rabbit was a bit overdone.'

'You are funny, Henry (pantomime). You mean the chicken! Yes, I quite agree, but the oven was on the hot side.' (It was an open grate!)

Silence for a while, then:

'Kindly pass me the salad, Henry.'

'The — ? Oh yes, sister, the salad.'

'Did you partake of sufficient of the apple pie, brother Henry?'

Now apple pie was Henry's seldom-enjoyed pet weakness and as he gazed sadly at the pile of skins on the table that represented the debris of his 'repast' his feelings became too strong for his discretion:

'Apple-pie? Apple-pie? Where the h— is the apple-pie? I saw d— all but a wheen o' praties an' a pickin' o' rabbit bones!'

Yes, 'Queen Anne' had her little eccentricities, and those who knew her well have often smilingly recalled them, but she was a loyal friend, was ever ready to help or sympathise with a neighbour in any trouble, and her passing at an early age caused widespread regret.

'Knockem's'

Lord Herbert Vane-Tempest, an uncle of Mr Winston Churchill, was the owner of Garron Tower until shortly before the 1914–18 war, when he sold it to a Larne hotel company, Messrs Henry McNeill, Ltd. This company, one of the pioneers of the tourist industry, ran charabanc and later omnibus tours from Larne to all the neighbouring places of interest, Garron Tower being almost always included in the itinerary.

Lancashire, Yorkshire and Cheshire people were circularised with attractive folders depicting our beauty spots, until it became an annual trip for thousands of English folk during 'Wakes Week'.

'Knockem's', as it was affectionately termed (the Main Street

Hotel, Larne) was a busy scene during this period. In addition to long distance tours by charabanc, with guides marshalling their charges into their places – 'Here y'are, sir! 'Knockem's' car, sir!' – the genial 'Knockem' himself (Henry McNeill) with his flowing, snowy side whiskers and his massive gold watch-chain well in evidence, could be seen arranging tours by jaunting car for those who preferred them. Freelance sidecar men also reaped a rich harvest during the holiday season, and frequently 'Knockem' had to engage their services to supplement his own large contingent of vehicles.

The story is told that one of his drivers was suspected by 'Knockem' of handing in rather less than his receipts after doing trips. One day 'Knockem' concealed himself in the stable, where the drivers were wont to count up their cash before handing it in.

The suspect entered, and after putting his horses in the stands, took his leather bag and started to count.

This is the monologue the listener heard:

'A bob for me, a tanner for 'Knockem'' – and so on until it came towards the end of the tally.

Here was a pause, then the voice went on, 'There's two bobs here. Should I give the bob to 'Knockem' or keep it myself?'

'Knockem' solved the problem! Showing his face over the side of the stand, he remarked mildly, 'Surely you'll give poor old 'Knockem' something for feeding the horses?'

It says a lot for 'Knockem' that he didn't sack the culprit and for years after his death there wasn't a more honest employee in the firm!

Ringfad

Ringfad is a low ridge of black rocks pointing across Carnlough

Bay towards Islandmagee and covered at high water. This point was the scene of a shipwreck in 1827 when a privateer returning from a profitable trip was driven ashore during a snow blizzard, and broke up, only a few survivors managing to reach the beach.

Many tales are told of the scenes when the local (Largy) residents gathered to help, actuated, no doubt, by humanitarian motives, and had their cupidity so much aroused by the valuable stuff coming ashore that in a kind of mass hysteria they even started cutting off the fingers and earlobes of the drowned victims to get the rings!

One of the rural poets who seem to always pop up at a time like this must have witnessed the horrible scene, and has immortalised it in a 'poem' called:

Loss of *The Enterprise*

The Enterprise of Lynn, brave boys,
It was our good ship's name;
She was laden with dollars and indigo,
And from Peru she came.
She crossed the western ocean,
Where foaming billows roar,
And left her precious cargo
Along the Largy shore.

'Twas on the 3rd of March, brave boys,
In the year of 'twenty-seven,
Our good ship through the dark and storm
Was by Glenarm driven.
The hail and sleet together met,

The spendrift it blew high,
Together with a fall of snow
And dreadful was the sky.
It was the captain's lady,
As I have heard them tell,
Had learned her navigation,
And she could use it well.

She took an observation
At twelve o'clock that day.
'I'll hold for fifty pounds,' says she,
'We're off Glenarm Bay.'

As we sailed by the Black Rock
A light it came in view.
'Oh, hold her off!' the Captain cried,
'Our lady's words are true.
Oh, hold her off for Greenock, boys;
Some danger we are near.'
But when we tried to put about,
Pale death did soon appear.

Oh, dark Ringfad, you held us fast
And would not let us go,
While every hill and valley round
Was covered deep in snow.
The seas ran high, none could come nigh
Our precious lives to save;
The Captain, wife and gallant crew
Soon found a watery grave.

Our mainmast falling overboard,
The rigging tore away,
Our noble ship in pieces went
Before the break of day.
Then on that Sabbath morning,
As daybreak did appear,
The people came from all around
To salvage from the gear.

Some silver plates and gold they got,
And other things beside,
Though captain, wife and all were left
A-rolling in the tide.
Then down came Johnny Murphy
And to the mate did say:
'Produce your landing order
For landing in our bay.'

The mate he scornful answered
And to Johnny Murphy said:
'Would you have landing orders
When such plunder you have made?
Our landing order it is lost
For to be found no more;
And see! My gallant shipmates
A-rolling on your shore.'

Then shame on Pat McLaughlin
And other folks as well,
Who stripped the riches off the dead,

As I heard people tell.
They cut the ears and fingers off
To get the rings and gold,
Then took their spoil to Carryreagh
And hid it in the mould

'Twas Martin, aye, and James Moorhead
Who took the dead away,
All covered with the salt sea wrack
And battered by the spray.
They left them by the Old Road side,
The truth I do declare,
Till everybody passing by
Took pity on them there.

A coroner's inquest was held
Some nine days since the wreck
To certify the bodies
That the sea had given back.
The mate was one among the few
Of them that did survive,
For out of crew of twenty-two
Not twelve were found alive.

Come all ye friends and neighbours,
The truth to you I'll tell,
It was up in McGalliard's
These men were treated well.
The captain, wife and company
When washed in by the tide,
Were brought to Nappan where they lie
In grave that's deep and wide.

Over fifty years ago, while cutting dulse at Ringfad a local man named Hunter lifted on his 'hook' a canvas sack full of Spanish doubloons. He got his treasure into the boat, but a year or two later another boatman wasn't so lucky! He hooked something, got it to the surface, and was just reaching over to grab it when the bottom dropped out of it, leaving him a rotten canvas bag but no gold!

To the southward of Ringfad is a lovely baylet or little cove, where silvery sand makes an ideal spot for bathing.

Few of the bathers know that they are standing or swimming over a treasure which at present values would fetch a colossal price could it be recovered – but maybe it is better left undisturbed, while the holiday-makers store up memories of bright sunshine, ozone-laden breezes and laughter, more valuable in their own way than any yellow metal.

The present Largy folk say that not one of the people concerned in the despoiling of the *Enterprise's* dead had good luck with his ill-gotten gains, and it is a fact that the only Largy residents who are descendants of anyone living there in 1827 are the McGalliards, who, as the ballad states, treated the dead with respect and the survivors with kindness.

There is no record of the valuable loot having been disposed of, so it may be that a large quantity of the stuff is still hidden in some 'sheugh' or souterrain at Carryreagh (pronounced Car-a-ree-ah).

Dungallon Fort

Dungallon, a hill overlooking the Largy, is supposed to have been the scene of one of the last battles fought by the Danes while making their way home after their disastrous defeat at Clontarf. In later times Dungallon was one of the spots where beacon fires were lit by the Antrim Scots when summoning the help or guiding the ships of their brethren from across the North Channel.

While we are up on Dungall let us look over towards Glenarm. What a glorious sight! Below us stretches Carnlough Bay, that lovely queen of all Antrim's bays that has been compared with the famous one of Naples.

Antrim's blue hills, ranging from near Larne to Glencloy on one side, and from Glencloy to the dark head of Garron on the other, enclose a sheet of water fringed with white sands that would be a mecca for holiday-makers in a less lavishly gifted land than ours.

To see it at its best, however, take a boat and row (or be rowed, if you are no oarsman) out to sea a couple of miles on a July morning, when the sun is just up over the horizon and the slight haze of opening day gives the land the appearance of a lovely lady awakening.

The white limestone cliffs, and even the scars left where the quarries have been worked, contrast with the many shades of green in fields and on tree-clad slopes.

The little burns, less boisterous than in the other seasons, show narrow silver ribbons bisecting the black rock at the mountain tops, and the wee village nestling cosily at the foot of Glencloy sends up its small plumes of smoke from newly-lit fires (some of it the 'blue reek' of peat).

Even so early as this, a sail or motor fisher may be seen creaming a track across the bay, a rattle of blocks or chug-chug of engine seeming in tune to the sound of our rowlocks or the swish of the water under our keel.

Carnlough

Ashore we had a bustling, busy, miniature town, clean and civic-conscious. Part of its prosperity came from the limestone quarries of the Carnlough Lime Company, ably managed by Mr Hugh S. Dempsey and Mr Millar, which exported the mineral per the little coasting craft, one of which was usually lying in the harbour, being loaded or maybe awaiting high water to sail for Glasgow, Garston or other port across Channel.

Not all of Carnlough's prosperity came from within: during times of depression it would have fared badly but for the money sent home by its sailormen! Carnlough, Glenarm – and Glenariff – have been famed, during the past century at least, for the quality of the seafarers they have bred.

In any trade, from the London–New Zealand to the Belfast–Garston, the sailor from Antrim's coast could be found, serving on deck, in engine room or stokehold, in spite of weather, water or war! Many wives were widowed, and children orphaned by the foul inventions of Kaiser Bill and Adolf Hitler's sea-war experts, who originated the cowardly 'sink without warning' attacks upon merchantmen, but despite all the fiendish tricks in their repertoire, the Glens seamen defied them. When the little ships were armed the reckless courage of their crews led to many an epic battle, when, outgunned and outranged, they closed in on their enemy and blew him out of the water!

The Carnlough Lime Company was a go-ahead concern, shipping limestone to Scotland for the ironworks, and also having a large trade in burned lime or whiting. A few years before the outbreak of the 1914–18 war a German-sponsored company started a peat works up on the mountainside above Carnlough, but after a short time it was suddenly abandoned. The site is still called 'The Peat Works'.

Our Waterfalls

The witchery of Irish waterfalls is well known. They have not the awe-inspiring grandeur of a Niagara or Zambesi fall, but for enchanting loveliness they are unequalled. Glenariff's waterfalls are named 'Ess-na-Larach', 'Ess-na-Crub', and other names which all but one ('The Tears of the Mountain') refer to a mare, 'The Fall of the Mare', 'The Fall of the Shoe', 'The Mare's Tail' and so on. Carnlough has its Doonan waterfalls and its Crannyburn, two little streams which fall over the rock in musical disorder, then sedately arrange themselves in regular cadence to continue, between fern-and-flower-decked fields, their journey seaward. Carnlough people love these falls and have a 'Waterfall Road' named after them.

The Doonan ('little fort') fall, attractive in itself, has an added attraction for those with antiquarian tastes, as it is near the Doonan Fort, an ancient burial tumulus which has at its base a number of huge stones forming large chambers.

Carnlough-born Miss N.J.N. Johnston, who was an authority on our ancient music and once Ulster's only Uilleann piper, lived here and Carnlough was also the home of several well-known literary men – Mr George Shiels, playwright, and the Rev. Aston Robinson, MA, the authority on the history of Ulster Presbyterianism. The late Professor Clarke Robinson, PhD, MA, BSc, though a native of Glenarm, ended his days here.

He received his first education at the hands of a schoolmaster named Patrick Magill, afterwards passing on to the Belfast Royal Academical Institution.

He showed a special aptitude for languages and literature and went from there to study at Bonn University where one of his fellow pupils was Prince Wilhelm, later Wilhelm II of Germany, the much hated 'I and God' Kaiser Bill of the 1914–18 war.

The 'Sliding Village'

One of the many wonders of the Antrim Coast is Straidkilly, the 'Sliding Village'. Straidkilly is forever depositing a large quantity of blue clay, basalt and limestone upon the coast road, at a spot almost midway between Carnlough and Glenarm, and labourers are needed the year round to shovel and wheel the stuff from the road. How long this miniature landslide has been going on is difficult to ascertain, but it is thought that (unless there is a natural arch in the rocks overlying the clay) there will eventually be a collapse of the central point, filling the space and forming another glen to add to the nine.

Straidkilly is supposed to have been the actual scene wherein was laid the first folk-tale about a human midwife for a fairy birth.

Several anachronisms appear to have been introduced, but allowing for the fact that it has been passed down by oral tradition from the earliest times, and differs little in material particulars from the Scandinavian folk tale, the story should be interesting. Here it is:

A certain woman, living in Glenarm Glen, had a wide reputation as a most successful midwife. One night, just as she was preparing for bed, she heard an urgent knocking at her door. Such knocks usually portended a call for her services, so she made haste to open and saw in the dim illumination that came from her rushlight a small figure about three feet or so high, dressed in driving clothes, and bearing a large whip.

'What is it?' she asked, looking at what she thought was a dwarf.

'Come, my good woman!' said the wee man, 'your services are needed and I have a coach waiting.'

'Where have I to go?' queried the midwife.

'Don't bother yourself about that!' answered the man impatiently. 'I tell you to hurry and you will be well paid.'

She did hurry, and when she was entering the vehicle she noticed that the doorway expanded to admit her, contracting after she had taken her seat, so that although she had plenty of room to sit comfortably, yet she felt she was imprisoned.

Only after what seemed a short drive the horses stopped, the driver dismounted and produced a piece of cloth with which he asked permission to blindfold her.

She was puzzled and even a bit alarmed by this request, but knowing that the midwife or the doctor were two people to whom violence was never offered, she submitted.

Taking her hand, her guide then led her into what seemed to be a cavern, judging by the drops of water that could be heard falling on either hand.

At last he stopped, removing the mask, and she found herself at the entrance to a lovely miniature castle whose many windows were blazing with light, though not a sound, except from one room, disturbed the stillness. To this room she was conducted.

Several hours later, after the safe arrival of a little boy, when the midwife had time to look around, she found that she was in a building whose every item showed that its tenants were fairies! Her patient was only between two and three feet high, though beautifully proportioned, and the baby was the smallest wee morsel she had ever seen.

She thought of going home again but when she went towards the outer door she found her way politely but firmly barred by two small doorkeepers who crossed the lances they carried as a stop sign.

One of them rang a bell and the driver of the previous night appeared and asked what was wrong. She explained that she wanted to have a run home, as she had chickens, a cow and a goat to see to.

'They are all being looked after,' he answered. 'But you must stay here for a couple of weeks until the Queen is up and about again.'

She was afraid to object to this order but on one point she was firm. Food must be brought to her from outside, not fairy food! (Anyone who eats food offered by fairies can be detained indefinitely by them, but if this is refused and ordinary human diet demanded, the fairies must supply it.) To this the wee people agreed and she was served with the best of eatables and drinkables during her stay.

A couple of days before the time set for her return home, she was bathing the baby, and anointing its head with some stuff supplied to her for the purpose, when her right eye started to itch. She put her hand up to rub it and in doing so a little of the ointment from her hand entered her eye.

Immediately she found herself back at home!

That it wasn't only a dream was proved by the fact that her neighbours asked her where she had spent the past fortnight, and also whether the lovely dumb girl who had looked after the place in her absence was a relation.

When she went to her bedroom, she found a large, golden-meshed purse lying on her pillow, full of golden coins and, when she went to the byre to milk, her surprise was great at seeing two cows instead of one and two goats tied to rings at the opposite wall!

The unusually loud cackling from the henhouse led her there

to investigate and she found that the number of her hens was exactly double what it used to be!

On her return to the house she happened to look at the dresser – and there was a row of bowls, each full of eggs.

The fairies had certainly kept their promise to repay her for her services, but one thing that puzzled her greatly was the connection the rubbing of her eye could have with the sudden termination of her fairyland visit.

Being of an easy-going nature she didn't let these strange happenings worry her, and took advantage of her new prosperity to visit Glenarm on a shopping expedition.

Walking into a shop where she intended to make some purchases, she was surprised to see a couple of wee people, with baskets over their arms, busy stuffing things from the counters into them, though the shopkeeper himself was in his kitchen and did not seem to know anything of the presence of his unorthodox customers.

'You surely aren't stealing those things?' she asked them, and at once the nearest one dropped his basket and confronted her.

'Can you see us?' he asked.

'Certainly,' said she.

'With both eyes?' he queried.

She put her hand over each eye in turn.

'No, only with the right eye,' she replied.

'Lucky for you!' said the wee man and with that he swung at her such a blow that she was ever afterwards blind of that eye!

To make matters worse, when she had the eye dressed and got home only one cow, one goat and the former number of hens were there, while on the table was a piece of paper with these words on it: 'When a blind eye sees again, your gold shall be found again in Straidkilly,' and sure enough all the gold had disappeared except what was in her pocket – amounting to exactly what she usually received for her fee!

Some day a person whose sight has been restored by some means or other will find the fairy gold in Straidkilly, if the story be true.

Coach Road to Glenarm

Over Straidkilly in the olden times there was a narrow bridle path. This was succeeded by a coach road which was for centuries – until the present coast road was built – the only highway around the Glens. It was rather a hazardous business, especially on a winter night, negotiating a stretch of road which might or might not have changed its course or possibly have collapsed in spots!

This road of a sort is still in existence and a few minutes' walk along it takes us to near Glenarm, one of the most history-steeped of the whole Nine Glens.

Glenarm – An Old Town

Glenarm is one of the oldest towns in all Ireland! It may look only a village but can boast of a Charter granted by King John (1199–1216) so that it has been a town for longer than our present cities of Belfast or Londonderry.

When John Bisset was outlawed in 1242 for the alleged participation in the murder of the Earl of Athol, he fled to Ireland where he received a grant of the 'Glynnes' (Glens) from the Earl of Ulster. Margery Bisset, sixth in descent from John, married John Mohr McDonnell and her husband got the appellation Lord of Dunyveg (Dunvegan, Skye) and the

Glynnes. In subsequent history his descendants figured prominently as when Sir John Chichester, writing in 1597, complained to Cecil, Lord Burghley, that besides being unable to get either rent or service from the McDonnell's, 'they had likewise broken down two of their castells, the one called Glinarme and the other Red Bawn (castle or fortification) forteffeing themselves only in Dunluce.'

Randal, First Marquis of Antrim, who had been active in the Civil War, was sent to the Tower in 1660 on suspicion of having opposed the Restoration. His production of a letter from the late King, Charles I, ordering him to take up arms, cleared him, and with the exception of advowsons (right of presentation to church livings) his rights and privileges were all restored to him.

The Castle

The original castle at Glenarm occupied a site on the opposite side of the river to the present building, the houses being built around it.

A good description of the castle is given in the *Dublin Penny Journal* of March 5, 1836. Here it is:

'The village itself contains nearly two hundred neat, whitened cottages; it is romantically situated by the shore side, in a deep ravine or sequestered glen, being closed in on either side by lofty hills and washed by the silvery waters of a mountain stream; on the opposite bank of which, in a commanding situation, stands the ancient castle, bearing the same name as the town and which for many years had been the residence of the Antrim family. In this direction also is seen the gracefully rising spire of the parish church – it stands on the beach, surrounded by a neatly-enclosed burying-ground. In the vicinity of the village is a finely wooded glen, leading to a little deer park, a place of singular construction, and well deserving the attention of the curious traveller…'

Perusing the old *Penny Journal* file again, we find the following description of an entertainment given in Antrim House, Merrion Square, Dublin, on April 3, 1794:

On Thursday night the mother of the late Marchioness of Antrim gave a most superb route, ball and supper, in this dwelling, to a very brilliant and extremely numerous assemblage of the first rank and fashion. His Excellency the Viceroy, and most of the nobility in town, were present.

'The grand Scots Ballet was on this occasion first performed by the following ladies: The Countess of Antrim, Lady Letitia M'Donald, Lady Isabella Beresford, Lady Anne Butler, Lady Augusta Forbes, Lady Theodosia Meade, both the Hon. Misses Gardiner, both the Misses Montgomery, Lady Leitrim, both the Hon. Misses Clements, Miss White, Miss Latouche, Miss Stewart, and Miss Ponsonby, now Countess Grey.

'The fair danseuses were in uniform dresses of white muslin, trimmed with blue ribbons, blue sashes, and petticoats trimmed with silver fringe – head dresses, white turbans, spangled with silver, and blue feathers. The music, which was all in the Scots style, was composed for the occasion. The ballet commenced with a strathspey in slow time and the figures of the dance varied with the tunes which had an excellent effect. The ballet, on its commencement, excited such admiration as to attract the whole company to the ballroom which scarcely allowed the charming performers to move. But by the polite and persuasive interference of the noble Marchioness the room was tolerably cleared and the press of the company restrained by barriers of ribbon held by noblemen…

How is that for a description of the way Dublin's nobility amused themselves while the last days of the Reign of Terror were keeping 'Madame Guillotine' busy in France, and Howe's squadron was moving into position to defeat the French fleet off Brest?

Shane O'Neill

Let us turn again to the historical background of Glenarm. The church the *Penny Journal* refers to is built on the site of a former Franciscan monastery, and there is a tradition that the body of 'Shane the Proud' (Shane O'Neill) is buried there (minus the head, 'spiked' at Dublin Castle). The story goes that a friar from Armagh came to Glenarm one day looking for the body so that it might be interred with those of his ancestors at Armagh. The Glenarm abbot considered a few moments then asked:

'Have you brought with you the remains of James McDonnell, Lord of Antrim and Cantire, who was buried among the strangers of Armagh?'

The friar, taken aback by this unexpected question, stammered, 'N-no.'

'Well then,' continued the abbot, 'whilst you continue to tread on James, Lord of Antrim and Cantire, know ye that we here in Glenarm will continue to trample on the dust of your great O'Neill!'

The yarn's a good one but its authenticity is more than doubtful, though the sentiment expressed by the Glensman reads true to type, as among the McDonnell Clan pride was both their strong point and their weakness.

It kept them from being assimilated properly into the framework of the race, yet caused them to be ready to resent the least slight – or fancied slight – to their family.

With such rulers over its destinies, Glenarm had its share in the turbulent history of Dalriada, but survived all the vicissitudes of internecine warfare, only to be almost wiped out in more modern and (ahem!) peaceful times.

August 1854

It is an August night in the year 1854. The big annual fair is on, having started that morning, and after the business of buying and selling is over for the day the people have gladly dropped money-making cares and are getting festive.

The dance houses are full, the light streaming from them, and the sound of music and revelry induces many other people to try the almost impossible feat of edging themselves into the midst of the fun. Light-hearted laughter rings out on the still air; but in the public-house to which one of these dance-houses is attached broods a very troubled publican.

He tries to hide his anxiety from his patrons, but with indifferent success, the cause of his worry being the fact that a Ballymena visitor who had lodged overnight in his house had died that afternoon, and the corpse was now lying in an adjoining room!

This was his dilemma: the fair was his best time for money-making business, and he knew that to allow the news to become general would cause people to avoid his establishment, if not to cease their merry-making altogether.

He decided to hold his tongue; but little did he know that his guest had died of cholera, and by the time he did know he was himself stricken.

The awful news spread rapidly, but hardly more quickly than the terrible disease, and all who had in any way had contact with the affected house were shunned. Doors were barred, the inmates of each house allowing nobody but members of their own family to enter.

These precautions were of little avail, for inside twenty-four hours almost every dwelling housed somebody who had the dread disease.

There wasn't as much wind as would shake a loose cobweb, which was a contributory factor in the spread of the pestilence, and people fled to the slopes overhanging the town, passing on their way the corpses of others who had succumbed while trying to escape.

The local physician at that time was named McAuley, and it is to his eternal credit that he did all it was humanly possible to do, from trying to stay the progress of the disease to preparing for interment the bodies of the dead. In this he was assisted by a brave cousin of the name Black.

One afternoon while engaging in this grisly task, the body which he was lifting into a sitting position belched some of the gases generated by its decay.

'I am finished!' Dr McAuley remarked in a calm voice to his assistant.

His words were prophetic, for he died next night.

His passing seemed to be the final sacrifice needed to end the awful tragedy. Those Glenarm folk, even the most timid, who were fit to be afoot at all, attended his funeral, and as the first shovelfuls were being thrown on the box which served as a coffin, a strong wind started to blow, and soon the deadly germs were cleared away.

Weeks after it was discovered that two fruit dealers, man and wife, had brought the disease with them from Ballymena, in some foreign fruit it was supposed.

Today there is a long, low mound at the back of the Church-yard wall, where it adjoins the main road, and within that mound lie the remains of the people who perished in the cholera epidemic.

Viewpoint from 'Madjie's Mill'

Up the New Road, as it is called, just above Glenarm, we arrive at 'Madjie's Mill', once the centre of Glenarm's corn milling, later a local place of assembly for ceilidh or dance, then filled in and built over for the new road. A few yards higher up we come to what is on a clear day one of the finest viewpoints in all Antrim (excluding Slemish top).

From the outer islands of Western Scotland down along its coastline past Cantyre, Bute, Ailsa Craig ('Paddy's Milestone') and Ayrshire down to Wigtownshire, all come within range of ordinary vision; on the left we have the green patchwork fields of the Largy, Garron Head – darker green from its many larch-treed slopes – and the point of Torr just hiding Rathlin.

To the right are the limestone cliffs, the low line of Islandmagee, and the twin rocks lying off it we call the 'Whullans' (a corruption of Cailini – colleens, hence 'Maidens') whose new and old lighthouses stand silhouetted against the sea beyond. Below us is Glenarm, its little limestone pier showing a steamer just casting off, then leaving a white wake across the bay as it starts its journey to Ayr, Troon, Ardrossan or Glasgow, loaded with iron ore or lime. Behind us the tree-fringed parklands of the Earl of Antrim stretch up along the little river until they merge with the bracken and heather. The Castle itself, partly concealed by trees, looks a lovely dwelling from here, and one could almost imagine it to belong to a more ancient period, and start weaving romances about its past – a past that really belongs to the castle once on this side of the river.

Many a joust or tournament was held down there in the days of chivalry, and many a noble knight ventured forth of its gates to do battle with an enemy, while within its walls fair ladies prayed for his safe return.

Nobility, Gentry and Bachelors!

The Earls of Antrim were always famed as good landlords, and the 12th Earl was no exception. Every movement that was for the betterment of the farming class had his support, and it was on June 15, 1932, only a fortnight after his return from Denmark, where he headed a delegation sent to examine Danish methods of dairying and pig-rearing, that he died.

He had succeeded in 1918 on the death of his father. His mother was a daughter of General the Hon. Charles Grey, and she was a member of Queen Victoria's Household, also an intimate friend of Her Majesty Queen Alexandra.

The 13th Earl of Antrim, lately deceased, married Angela, daughter of Sir Mark Sykes Bart., in 1934, and there are three children. His Lordship showed his interest in the townspeople by establishing a furniture factory during the depression years. In the 1938-45 war, Messrs Gallaher, the Belfast tobacco firm, took over the premises for use in the manufacture of their products, and many people from Glenarm and the surrounding districts were employed there. His Lordship served at sea during the war of 1939-45, becoming a Lieut. Commander RNVR.

Lady Antrim was most energetic in furtherance of all schemes of assistance to the war effort, and found time to help the Gibraltarian evacuees who were housed in 'tin-towns' at Broughshane, Glenravel, Moorfields, Crossgar, Ballyarnett, and several other places in Counties Derry, Antrim and Down. She arranged exhibitions of their work and encouraged them to busy themselves at handicrafts. When the war ended in Europe and the liberated peoples were looking to these Isles for succour, her Ladyship headed one of the parties which (under UNRRA) went across to help. Starting operations in Holland, they quickly won golden opinions from the Dutch, and their efforts resulted in many persons being helped on the way to a new peace-time existence. A gifted sculptress, Lady Antrim used her scant free time to model some of the people she met, notably a Jewess mother and child.

There are few places the size of Glenarm that can boast of so many notabilities born there – James McNeill, President of the (then) Irish Free State; Judge Campbell, of the US judiciary and Professor Eoin McNeill, the noted Gaelic scholar, were natives of the wee town, and we may claim that John Clarke ('Benmore'), the poet and antiquary, became a Glenarm man, while his birth at Cairncastle permits us to claim that David Manson, the famous dominie, was a near-Glenarm man.

2

Famous People and Characters

Before we go any further let us learn a little of the history of some of the famous people and 'characters' who once lived in these parts.

The McDonnells

Glenariff, as we have already seen, was one of the strongholds of the Clan McDonnell, and in later years the surviving descendants of the clan built themselves a large mansion (Ballinluig, later owned by Senator Joseph Maguire) where they continued to live in semi-regal state for a long time.

At the end of the eighteenth century a branch of the family migrated to Dublin, where its members figured largely in the gay social life of the capital, but it remained for scions of a less-wealthy branch to gain fresh laurels for the name of McDonnell.

One of these, a son of Michael McDonnell, was Dr James McDonnell, founder of the first Fever Hospital in Great Britain or Ireland, and prime mover in the organisation of the famous Harp Festival in Belfast (1792), a meeting of native musicians at which the last ten survivors of the once-numerous Irish harpers played music which was noted down by Edward Bunting, whose collection embodies the best of what remains of our ancient melodies.

James McDonnell, born in the year 1762, received his early education in one of the caves at Red Bay, where he was taught by a schoolmaster named Maurice Traynor. From there he went to Belfast, was prepared for the University by David Manson, then went to Edinburgh, where he graduated in Medicine in 1784. He quickly made a name for himself in his profession, and was chosen by many of the well-off burgesses of Belfast as the family physician, being also consulted by his fellow-practitioners in difficult cases.

Despite his many other duties, Dr McDonnell found time to devote to the betterment of the condition of the poor and labouring classes (synonymous terms at that time!) and it was largely due to his efforts that the Belfast Charitable Institution was so well organised that it has lasted down to our day.

By an odd chance, when the air raids on Belfast necessitated the evacuation of the Institution's inmates to safer surroundings, Garron Tower, only a few miles from McDonnell's birthplace, was chosen as their wartime home.

Another achievement of Dr McDonnell was the establishment of the first fever hospital in Great Britain or Ireland. Belfast, in common with all other large towns of the period, was terribly fever-ridden, typhus especially almost decimating the population at times, and the doctor decided that new methods of dealing with the scourge were necessary.

He convened a meeting of public-spirited citizens on April 14, 1797, at which a committee was appointed to arrange for the acquisition of premises suitable for treatment of fever. A house in Berry Street was rented at £20 per annum, on April 27 it was opened for the reception of patients, and by June 1, ten severe fever cases had been cured and discharged.

Thus was founded the Belfast Dispensary and Fever Hospital, the forerunner of the Royal Victoria Hospital, and thus was established a tradition that has stimulated Belfast-trained doctors and surgeons to retain their place in the forefront of medical and surgical research.

After the unsuccessful rebellion of 1798, among those tried and executed was Henry Joy McCracken. McCracken was hanged in front of what was then the Belfast Jail at Corn Market, and as soon as possible after he had been 'turned off' (to use the expression current at the time) some of his relatives got the body and hurried with it to Dr McDonnell's, hoping he might be able to resuscitate it.

Dr James was away from home, so his brother Alexander (also a doctor) undertook the task, but without success.

This restoring of the apparently hanged had been performed on several occasions by doctors in England, as the method of execution caused death by strangulation, and not, as at present, by dislocation of the vertebrae. It was tried, but in vain, when Dr Dodd was hanged in 1777 for forgery.

In the north-west corner of the ancient graveyard at Layde, Cushendall, stands a splendid Celtic cross, bearing the following inscription:

> Erected in memory of James McDonnell, of Belfast and Murlough, in this county; a Physician whose great abilities and greater benevolence made him venerated in the Glens of Antrim, where he was born, and in Belfast, where he died AD 1845, in his 82nd year.
>
> Also in memory of Eliza, daughter of John

Clarke, Esq., of Belfast, and wife of the said James McDonnell; she died AD 1798.

Also of Penelope, daughter of James Montgomery, Esq., of Larne, and second wife of the said James McDonnell; she died AD 1851.

Also in memory of Michael, father of the said James, and of Alexander, father of Michael, and of Coll, father of Alexander, and son of Major-General Sir Alexander Coll McDonnell, Knight of the Field, whose other son, Captain Archibald McDonnell, likewise rests in this churchyard.

Another inscription in Layde records:

> Here lies the remains of Coll McDonnell, of Kilmore, Glenariff, who died 25th March, 1719. Son to Major-General Sir Alexander McDonnell (MacCollcito) by his loving wife, daughter of McAlister, Laird of Laup.
>
> Sir Alexander, celebrated in the wars of Montrose in Scotland, was slain 13th November, 1647, while 2nd in command of the Royal Forces at Knockononess, and is buried at Clonmeen, County Cork.

This Sir Alexander McDonnell, or 'Colkitto' as he was called in Scotland, led three regiments of Irishmen (in 1644) across to Scotland, and in the subsequent battles from Tippermuir, Perth, to Kilsyth (1645) contributed largely to any victories gained.

The Layde Graveyard in which these tombstones stand was

at one time the site of a Franciscan monastery, founded about 1250, and then was for some time a Protestant church, but only part of the original or later buildings is standing.

David ['Master'] Manson

David Manson, one of the pioneers of modern education, was born in 1726, the son of John Manson, of Cairncastle.

As a child he was weakly, and when at eight years of age he developed rheumatic fever it left him with an enfeebled frame for the rest of his life.

Prevented from participation in the athletic pursuits of the ordinary child, he devoted himself to study, and soon acquired local fame not only for his scholarship, but also for his power of inspiring others to acquire learning.

The tenant of nearby Ballygally Castle was a Mr Shaw, who engaged David Manson as a tutor for his children. The young tutor must have been a godsend to the little Shaws, as he was no believer in the 'Spare the rod, spoil the child' adage that was adduced as an excuse by the 'Wackford Squeers' type of schoolmaster then prevalent.

He then launched out as a schoolmaster ('qualified to impart knowledge in all subjects' a contemporary advertisement declared) at Ballycastle, and later on in England, whence he returned to marry a Ballycastle girl, Miss Lynn.

In 1754, aged 28, he went to reside in Belfast, which had at the time a population of about 9,000 and the *News-Letter* of October 17, 1755, carried this advertisement:

'David Manson, at the request of his customers having opened an evening school in Clugston's Entry, teacheth by way of amusement English grammar, reading and spelling at a moderate expense.'

In five years he had established himself as Belfast's leading 'dominie', and had to remove from Clugston's Entry to a more spacious schoolroom in High Street.

The Hamiltons

Elizabeth Hamilton was the author of *The Cottagers of Glenbirnie* and was a former pupil of Manson's, and mentioned her old teacher in terms of affection and respect in the book.

In addition to *The Cottagers* she wrote *Letters of a Hindoo Rajah*; *Modern Philosophers*; *Letters on the Elementary Principles of Education*; *Life of Agrippina*; *Exercises on Religious Knowledge*, and *Popular Essays*. She was an intimate friend of Maria Edgeworth (1767–1849), whose stories of Irish life, *Castle Rackrent*, *The Absentee*, etc., are true pictures of the period described.

Miss Hamilton's brother Charles, also an ex-pupil of Manson's seminary, was author of a *Translation of the Hedija*, was praised by the famous Warren Hastings, and had a tablet to his memory erected in the vestibule of Rosemary Street Presbyterian Church, Belfast.

Nannie's Cave

Now let us retrace our steps to the red sandstone caves at Red Bay, where for fifty years lived Ann Murray, prototype of 'Oonagh of the Cave' in Banim's *Boyne Water*.

There is no record of what induced Ann (or 'Nannie' as she was called locally) to choose the cave as a dwelling-place (houses, if not very good, were plentiful) but at any rate she lived there from her 50th year until her death at the ripe-ish age of over 100 years!

Somewhere about 1796 Ann arrived at Waterfoot, and after

a few days spent in roaming around the district she got into the habit of spending some of her time in the blacksmith's forge (then situated in the cave nearest the village).

As the smith's fire kept his place fairly warm and dry, it is likely that Nannie came to the conclusion that cave no. 2 could also be made comfortable.

Shortly after she had settled in, the rumour spread that she kept a good 'drop o' the crathur', or 'mountain dew' or 'poteen' if you want to be exact, and soon her 'shebeen' was doing what was literally a 'roaring' trade!

Travelling in those times wasn't the simple thing it has since become, and many a weary traveller was glad to wet his whistle with Nannie's brew after negotiating the narrow track that was the only highway around the Antrim coast, or over the hills from Ballymena.

Mr and Mrs S.C. Hall, who toured Ireland in the early part of the last century, thus described her visit to Nannie's abode about 1840:

'Her swollen person and appearance suggested to us a resemblance to the toads which are found imbedded in the sandstone rocks, and which thrive without air; from the blackened ceiling of her 'den' the heavy damps distilled in huge drops, while the smoke struggled to escape through the door, and the room was reeking with the smell of poteen.'

The Halls (somewhat tactless, was it not?) asked Nannie if Father Matthew (a great temperance advocate of that day) had visited her. Her reply, given with some asperity, was:

'He might go where he was wanted, which wasn't just there – the quality always took a drop of her spirits as they passed. Why not – and in troth, it wasn't safe to be without it.'

67

The travellers then asked 'what safety could be endangered by its absence?' to which Nannie's reply was: 'Setting a case of shipwreck – for all the water looks so safe now, it's stormy enough betimes. I mind the time when the scream of drowning life was louder than the wind, or the beating of the sea either. And then I've gone out with my drop of comfort and poured betwixt lips that you'd think would never speak a word of love again, and it has brought them back to the world we're all so loath to leave, though we don't care to say so – or suppose,' she added, 'a gintleman felt a weakness about his heart, it would be a poor case if Nannie had nothing to put the strength in him again – or if a storm overtuck the traveller in Red Bay, wouldn't it be a disgrace if he couldn't find comfort as well as shelter in its covers?'

'The biggest payment I ever got,' she continued, 'was from one that hadn't a halfpenny to give me. A poor sailor's wife and her babby were washed ashore on a beam, or something, and a blow from a stone knocked the life out of the mother for a while, and yet she still clasped her child. I rolled the babby up in a blanket, and fed it, and it fell asleep. The mother was a long time coming to herself, but when she did come, the screech she gave out for her child would have pierced through stone hearts, and nothing could persuade her it wasn't drowned, until I laid it soft and rosy, and sleeping, by her side.

'Then the poor thing blessed me again and again: she'd fall asleep blessing and wake blessing; and I think the sound of them blessings has never left the echoes of Red Bay from that day to this – they were great payment intirely.'

That illustration of the real Nannie caused the Halls to add: 'We were sorry we had likened old Nannie to a toad, but consoled ourselves with thinking that she wore the 'precious jewel' in her heart instead of on her head.'

Poor Nannie's own life was not without tragedy. She had a son, and it is told locally that he was murdered, while still in his teens, by a half-witted man named Henry Lucas, who attacked him with a hatchet on the road over Crookanavick.

During her tenancy of her cave home she was visited – as she herself truthfully boasted – by most of the nobility of Great Britain and Ireland, and even by a few foreign potentates, and it was after studying her way of life that Banim created 'Oonagh of the Cave', one of the characters in his *Boyne Water*.

In 1847, one of the famine years, Nannie died, aged over 100, and was buried in the ancient graveyard at Kilmore, near the remains of what is said to have been one of the first churches founded by St Patrick.

Famous Glens Navigators

Another native of Glenariff who made history – sailing-ship history – was Capt. Charles McDonnell, once master of the famous clipper *James Baines*.

Charles McDonnell, who belonged to a branch of the same family as the Dr James McDonnell whose story we have already related, was born at Ballymellagh, Glenariff, in 1828. He attended Talmaght School, taught by a certain George Doran, a man destined to play a large part in his pupil's later success.

As soon as he was old enough, Charles McDonnell shipped in one of the little schooners which traded into Red Bay, and quickly became a capable seaman – no easy task in the days of 'wooden ships and iron men'! His proficiency soon gained him a berth in one of the crack lines, and he was only in his early twenties when he gained his 'ticket' (master's certificate) and was appointed first mate of the *Marco Polo*, then commanded by Captain J.N. Forbes ('Bully' Forbes of sea-ballads), whom he succeeded as master of that world-renowned vessel.

A fearless navigator, McDonnell distinguished himself by his treatment of his crew, who appreciated a more human officer after the 'hazing' they had had at Forbes' hands, and reacted accordingly. When McDonnell's ship was in Liverpool, and the word was passed round that she needed a crew, volunteers were always available, and 'shanghai-ing' was never needed!

During his spell as chief officer of the *Marco Polo* he received a gold watch of which he was very proud. It was inscribed: 'Presented to Mr Charles McDonnell by the owners of the *Marco Polo*, as their testimony of their high opinion of his services as chief officer when she made her unparalleled passage of 68 days to Melbourne, and 78 days home, the voyage, including detention, being completed in five months twenty-one days.'

In 1853, James Baines, of Liverpool, owner of the 'Black Ball' Line, decided to have some faster ships built to compete in the Australian trade. Donald McKay, of Boston, had a good name in shipbuilding circles, so Baines chose him as designer and builder, a choice which McKay justified by building in the years 1853–54 the four clippers *James Baines*, *Champion of the Seas*, *Donald McKay* and *Lightning*, all of which made their mark in clipper-ship history.

McDonnell, to his great delight, was appointed master of the *James Baines*, launched on July 25, 1854, and in September 1854, she left Boston for Liverpool where she arrived in 12 days 6 hours.

The shipping newspapers were full of accounts of her arrival; Liverpool's shipowners and any shipmasters in port flocked to inspect her, and all voted her the finest sailing ship Mersey had ever seen.

She was of 2,275 tons, measuring 266 feet overall, by 46.8 beam and 31 feet depth of hold; and a slight idea of her size may be got from the fact that her main yard was 100 feet long, she carried skysail stunsails and a main moonsail, her spread of canvas being 13,000 yards.

Her first 'long' passage was Liverpool–Melbourne, which she did in 63 days 18 hours, McDonnell being heard to remark, 'If I only had had the ordinary run of winds I would have done it in 55 days.'

Even so, on this trip her best day's sail, 423 miles, with main skysails and stunsails set, was only 13 miles less than the record established by her sister-ship, the *Lightning*! She completed the round-the-world passage in 132 days – a record.

A certain amount of the credit for the achievements of Captain McDonnell must be given to George Doran, who taught him the first principles of navigation, and afterwards helped the young officer by his advice.

McDonnell, during any home leave he had, was in the habit of consulting Doran, and it is believed that this obscure country schoolmaster was first to propound the theory of 'Great Circle Sailing' which his pupil afterwards put into practice.

The story is told that McDonnell lost a £100 wager which he had with a captain on the same route. He wagered that even if the other man's ship left twenty-four hours before the *James Baines*, he could overtake, pass her and be first into port. When he told Doran of his disappointment, George asked to be shown the courses followed. McDonnell gave him the information; the old dominie plotted a new set of courses, handed them over with the remark, 'Wager £200 this time' – and when the opportunity came the *Baines* won hull down!

In the year 1856 the following entries appeared in the log of the *James Baines*: June 16th: At noon sighted ship in distance ahead; at 1 p.m. alongside her; at 2 p.m. out of sight astern.

(The *Baines* was doing 17 knots, and the other vessel was the *Libertas*, bowling along under double-reefed topsails.)

Any old sailing-ship man can imagine the scene, going at 21 knots in a gale from south to sou'-west, with the main skysail set, in the 'Roaring Forties'.

It took courage to carry that press of canvas, but McDonnell had courage, as witnessed the time when he was tacking so close to Mizen Head that some of the passengers remonstrated. He only smiled, and replied, 'We must make a good passage!'

At the time of the Indian Mutiny (1857) the *James Baines* was commissioned as a troopship, and at Portsmouth Queen Victoria herself came to inspect the ship of whose performances she had heard so much. The story goes that when her Majesty was received aboard by McDonnell, she asked his name. Instead of saying, 'Charles McDonnell, your Majesty', his reply was, 'Captain McDonnell!'

'A very good name,' was the Queen's acknowledgement – and thus he lost the knighthood she had intended to confer upon him!

Whether his luck turned some time after cannot be definitely known, but we do know that his time of 101 days was poor in comparison with the *Lightning's* 87 days, though later passages showed that it was not inferior seamanship was to blame.

In 1858, the *James Baines* arrived in Liverpool with a cargo of jute, rice, linseed and hides and on April 22, when the hatches were opened, she was found to be on fire.

All other methods of extinguishing the outbreak having failed, an attempt was made to scuttle her (letting the water into the hold until she sank) but instead of sinking she only went aground, in the Huskisson Dock, and was burned to the water's edge.

The loss of his beloved ship was a severe blow to McDonnell, who returned home to Glenariff. During the winter of 1858 a small schooner was seen to be floundering off Ardclinis. Hurrying to where preparations were being made to effect a rescue, he took charge, himself going out in a small boat to the wreck, and being responsible for the saving of several lives. He received a severe wetting, did not change his clothes owing to his preoccupation with further rescue efforts, contracted pneumonia, and died after a short illness.

In the home of his grand-nephew, Mr Charles McDonnell, Kilmore, Glenariff, there are preserved some most interesting mementoes of the famous navigator. One, a painting of a ship off Land's End, was presented to him by shipowner James Baines himself; another, a service of plate, bears the inscription 'Presented by the Saloon Passengers of the Ship *James Baines* as a Mark of Esteem to Commander Charles McDonnell, May, 1855.'

At the little graveyard in the Milltown may be seen the following inscription upon a tombstone: 'Captain Charles McDonnell, late Master of the packet ship *James Baines*, of the Australian Line, who departed this life 26th January, 1859. Aged 31 years.'

And so, within sound of the sea he loved, the sea over whose expanse, from England to Australia, he had sailed in defiance of some of its wildest moods, he lies in peace.

Perhaps it was better that he should have passed on before the beautiful white-winged queens of the ocean were superseded by those smoky, horrible atrocities the sail-and-steamers, from which ugly ducklings were evolved the smart steam or oil-propelled vessels of today.

The *Queen Mary* or *Queen Elizabeth* may be – according to modern ideas are – beautiful also, but the old sailing-ship man still thinks of the clipper-ship period as the heyday of sail, of beauty in ship modelling, and of ocean travel.

McDonnell was not the only man who kept alive the Glens' tradition for fearless seamanship. A contemporary of his, Dennis Black, also of Kilmore, sailed with 'Bully' Forbes, and the following letter, dated January 8, 1858, gives some idea of Forbes' treatment even of his officers:

Ship *Young Mechanic*, Bombay

My Dear Uncle

I hope you will forgive me for not writing sooner. I suppose you have heard of the *Hastings* on her voyage from Morton Bay to Bombay, having to put in to Sydney in a sinking state. From thence I full intended to write to you, and was in the act of doing so when I found that some of the crew were trying to desert the ship. The Captain being on shore, I placed them in irons and had to watch them nearly all night in place of writing.

Shortly after arriving here I took my discharge from Captain Forbes, as we were not agreeing very well; in fact, he tried to injure me all he properly could here and get me out of Mr Baines's employ. I know the reason of all this: it has been arranged some time past, but perhaps it's best you should not know the reason at present. Captain Forbes is likely to be out here two or three years and I am clear of him. I wish to say no more about him, for I'm afraid there are too many speaking against him.

'Captain Forbes thought that when I left him that I should have to ship before the mast [i.e. as an ordinary seaman, not an officer], but he was a little surprised when he heard that I was chief officer of I may say the finest looking ship in the harbour, an American ship, 1,400 tons, and not unlike the *Lightning*. I have no desire to sail in American ships, but there is no choice here at present, as there are mates shipping nearly every day before the mast.

'The *Young Mechanic* will leave here about the 20th of this month for Hull, and I hope to be on English ground about the latter end of April.'

A letter from Liverpool, dated August 5, 1858, says:

'... I have been Chief Officer of the ship *Hope* for the last ten days. She is a fine ship between 11 and 12,000 tons register. She leaves here tomorrow for Cork, and from there on the 10th for Bombay with troops ... I had a very pleasant time in Jersey (he had an uncle there) and had the pleasure of seeing the Queen and upwards of 20,000 soldiers reviewed on my return to London ...'

A letter headed: Ship *Alipore*, London Dock, January 22, 1862, says:

'... We arrived yesterday from Bombay, and I may say we had a favourable passage home, much longer than I expected when I left. The ship has been very leaky from the Equator, and were it not for the assistance rendered by the troops we would have been obliged to run for the first port...'

Later, when Master of the *Alipore*, she was posted missing after a hurricane which raged while she was on an outward passage, and her loss had to be presumed, as not even wreckage that could be identified as belonging to her was ever found.

The fate of many such fine vessels is unknown, but neither the 'ordinary' hazards of seafaring nor the worst that 'frightfulness' of an enemy could invent have ever deterred Glensmen from roaming the seven seas, 'in sail' from the full-rigged beauty to the schooner, and 'in steam' from the 'mast-and-a'half' coaster to the Blue Riband liner.

It was a coaster skipper, Captain McKeegan, who commanded the last British vessel to leave Germany after war had been declared in 1914, and rather an adventurous passage he had, slipping out from Hamburg to the open sea! During the Spanish Civil War another Glensman, Captain Walsh, ran the blockade time and again while in command of the *Portalet*, and during the last war with Germany several Nine Glens natives received decorations and mention in the Gazette for their courage when attacked by German ships or aircraft.

Many of these sailors will return no more, but while it continues to wash the shores of the Antrim Coast young eyes will ever turn towards the sea, where adventure calls, where Father and/or Grandfather spent most of a lifetime, where some have achieved fame, a few (very few!) fortune, and where the days and night of unremitting battle with the elements can give a lad not only a rolling gait, but also a come-hither look in his eye few beauteous damsels can resist!

Some Local Poets

As befits a spot so full of beautiful scenery, the Glens district has inspired quite a number of poets, but of the purely local variety the principal ones were Alex ('Poet') McKie, Dan McGonnell, James Studdert Moore ('Dusty Roads the Tramp' he called himself) and James Gorman. These four delighted in the bardic style of narrative extolling the virtues or castigating the failings of their neighbours.

No big event, such as a regatta, horse-race, show or public meeting was held without some of these ballad-makers composing a 'poem' describing it in detail, and woe betide the luckless wight whose behaviour did not meet with their approval.

Poet McKie, who claimed to have been at a time in the 'Horse Police' in Belfast, was, when I met him first, a tall, gaunt figure of a man, striding along with both arms describing semi-circles in front of his chest, the while he declaimed a 'varse' or two from his latest composition. 'Huh! The Poet was a boy in his young days!' was a favourite exclamation of his, and from all accounts he was too!

When the *Peridot*, a coaster belonging to Messrs Robertson of Glasgow, was lost with all hands, Poet McKie recorded the disaster in a many-line poem that is still remembered, while his *Montgomery* – the story of the tragic loss of three young men during a boat race at Cushendall – was adapted to an old air, and is still sung round winter firesides.

Dan McGonnell, 'the Butcher Bard of Lurigedan', was a butcher to trade, but found time for the composition of numerous descriptions in rhyme of local happenings. His *Courting of Henry Pat* is in its own way a classic, and his *Glenarm Regatta* is still a favourite recitation whenever gig-racing enthusiasts get together, while for rollicking fun *The Skipper of the Ice Cream Shop* is hard to beat.

Dan got the idea for the *Ice Cream Shop* from an incident in which he and a crony figured in their younger days. They had been enjoying some 'refreshments' in a Carnlough pub, and with elevated minds decided to visit an ice cream vendor whose establishment was close to – and partly over – the river or burn that flows through the village.

The crack was so good here a while that they did not notice that a terrific storm of wind and rain was raging outside, but had a rude reminder when the suddenly swollen river came surging against the flimsy wooden structure they occupied and swept it away into mid-stream!

There wasn't much danger, and after his first fright the sobered Dan clambered out and, followed by the owner of the shop, waded through the few feet to the shore, but his chum elected to remain with the 'ship', and did in fact stay there until the flood subsided.

James Studdert Moore – 'Dusty Roads' to his intimates – was a most original type of character. Born near Cushendall, he left home very young, joined the army, was a few years in sailing ships, then returned to his native place, married, and attempted to settle down. Finding this settling-down business irksome, he 'took the bag for it', as it is euphemistically described locally, and tramped around the country, composing poems during his travels and reciting them as payment for services rendered, a payment which was deemed quite adequate by the people whom he favoured by his visit.

He was no beggar in the accepted sense of the word, and I have seen him rise and leave a house with a cheery 'Good day to yis all!' when nothing was offered to him, or keep his pipe pocketed lest it be seen that his supply of 'weed' was exhausted. He carried a blacking tin, with a bootlace strung through a hole in the side of it, and when asked the time would appear to consult this odd watch, his reply being, however, remarkably close to Greenwich reckoning!

A few people, realising that here was a genius, if erratic, tried to get him to settle down and write for a living. One weekly newspaper took him in charge for a while, but the call of the highway was too strong, so he donned the rags and 'took at it' again.

He died aged about 95, leaving behind him a number of old tattered copy books in which he had written his poems. Several of these compositions would not have disgraced some of the much-lauded poets of last century, while all are above the level that we associate with the country versifier.

Here are the names of a few: *Death Song of Saga-We-Watha; Fallaghmmacrilly; The Rock of Dunmaul; Robin Kennedy, The Smith of Tiveragh; Vale of Glenaan; Carey Lough, or The Lord of Dunluce; The Pibroch of Gordon; Song of Myself; The Battle of Aura; Turkish War Song; The Wedding of Donal Delargy; A Catastrophe; Ballycastle Bay; Rathlin Island* and there are many others.

His versatility was amazing. He could switch from a Turkish

love song to a song of the '98 Rebellion, or a poem descriptive of the beauties of his homeland, and his thoughts flowed with equal facility in each. Take these few lines as examples:

from *To Kathleen*

> Had I a regal throne, or a palace of my own,
> 'Tis thee, and thee alone, should be my queen;
> There, seated by my side, I would gaze on thee with pride,
> My bonnie Irish bride, Kathleen.

from *The Rock of Dunmaul*

> The Rock of Dunmaul, it is sanctified ground,
> 'Twas there that the King of Ulidia was crowned;
> The prince of each province, the Ard Righ and all,
> Received their gold crowns on the Rock of Dunmaul.

from *Turkish War Song*

> Sons of Islam, arise! There is danger at hand,
> Remember the promise our Prophet hath given –
> Who dies by the sword in defence of our land
> Shall share with the houris the pleasures of Heaven.

The following poem has its scene at Carey Lough, the 'Dark Loughareema' of Moira O'Neill's poem:

> The Lord of Dunluce to the hunting is gone,
> The hare and the wild deer his quarry;

He hunted o'er brake, o'er moorland and lawn,
Till he came to the loughs of Carey.
In Ireland's wide zone there is no spot so lone,
On Antrim's blue hills none so dreary;
The East winds there moan o'er the moss-covered stone,
The sound of the tempest is eerie.
Down from his horse sprang the Lord of Dunluce,
And down sprang his huntsmen so merry,
With 'Here will we stay till the sun's latest ray
Disappears o'er the far hills of Derry.'
Then up and outspake an old huntsman: 'I pray
Dear master of mine, be you wary,
And do not thou stay till the dawn of the day
By the fearsome dark lough of Carey.
'For out of that lough comes a spirit of guile,
In guise of fair young maiden,
With languishing lance and roseate smile,
Gay garments her lithe limbs arrayed in.
'And woe to the bouchal this maiden admires,
If he for a season should tarry;
His heart is consumed by love's fierce inward fires,
He wanders distraught over Carey.'
'Ha! An old wife's tale,' said the Lord of Dunluce,
''Tis little I heed and less fear it;
I would build me a hut if the winds make truce,
And a spirit would ne'er come near it.
'So build me a bothy of hazels grey,
And cover it over with heather,
And there I will bide by the lone lough side,
I and my huntsmen together.'

They built him a bothy of hazels grey,
They covered it o'er with heather,
And there he abode till the dawn of day,
With his merry men together.
Not an eye but his own beheld her that night,
When she called him forth from the shieling,
Not an eye beheld – the unholy sprite,
And Dunluce at her white feet kneeling.
'Swear to be mine, thou Lord of Dunluce,
White water flows thro' Carey river.'
He swore to be hers with a terrible oath,
While water flows through Carey river;
Then she prest his pale lips with the kiss of death,
And Dunluce was hers for ever.
His men wrapped his corpse in cerements white,
While caoining was Maeve Delargy;
They carried him forth at the dead of the night,
Now he rests in the beds of Margy.
And ever since then, when the moon's pale rays
Light a world in silence sleeping,
Is seen that sprite by the bosky braes,
And Dunluce at her side a-weeping.

James Gorman, the son of a schoolmaster who became 'captain' in the Glenariff ore mines, was born in the district, but spent many years in Belfast before transferring from there to the Scottish railway service, which he left on pension.

During his sojourn in Glasgow many of his compositions appeared in Ulster newspapers, and when he went to live at Falavee after his retirement he found more time to devote to his hobby. He was a well-read and most intelligent man, and his comments on passing people and events were well worth listening to, either in prose or verse.

He had the happy knack of extracting fun out of even a commonplace incident, giving it the twist that changed it from the ordinary to the comic as witnessed in his *Hiker's Lament*, or the *Lines on a Shark*. At the suggestion of some of the 'playboys' in Cushendall he wrote *The Swankers of Sweet Cushendall*, which proved a hit wherever it was sung, and his *Lament for Alex, the Gander of Cromac Square, Belfast* caused great amusement when published.

Many readers will remember the gander and geese that once roamed undisturbed in and about Cromac Square, Belfast. Many a time – and particularly on Friday, market day – have I seen these lordly birds, led by 'Alec', strutting across the Square, dodged by farm carts, cabs and even slowing the progress of tramcars! In later years, when traffic became denser, and sudden acceleration was necessary to make up for time lost in 'jams', the geese found life precarious and disappeared, whether by accident or the demands of the table is not known. Here, however, is part of the story of the gander:

This popular bird was well-known in the Square,
His nickname was Alec, his virtues were rare;
The favourite of ev'ry conductor and driver,
Who wouldn't have parted with him for a fiver.
'Twas known that Alec was fond of a drink,
Which lessened his caution, as most people think;
His favourite 'wet' was the brew of the Liffey,
And a 'big lift' was lowered by him in a jiffy.

Poor Alec one time went a little too far,
And had on his 'false face' before leaving the bar;
It was seen as he waddled all over the street
In a manner that showed he was most indiscreet.
But a bus came along and it flattened him out,
To the horror of those who were standing about;
And rumours of suicide spread, so I'm told,
'Cause his mate had that morning been plucked, trussed, and sold.

After a few well-deserved lines of eulogy, the poem concludes
on a note of warning:

> That if Alec had drunk from his own Cromac Springs,
> He'd be living and happy and flapping his wings.

James Kelly, who spent most of his early years at Cut Rock,
Garronpoint, but is now living in Glenarm, has composed
several pieces which show that he has the versifier's gift, coupled
with a keen sense of humour. Here is one of his poems which is
representative:

Love and the Mountain

On the fourteenth of September, a bright and sunny day,
Across the Garron mountain a pair of lads did stray,
Accompanied by two sisters I'll mention not by name,
But weren't they the sorry four when they came back again!
How many hours they did stay there I won't exactly say,
But when the golden sun set in the west, which meant the close
of day.

And when the time came to descend, a-down the hill they went,
Their hearts enraptured with their love and love's own sweet
content.
But when they reached the mountain-foot their joy and pride did
fall,
For pa and ma awaited them close by the garden wall.
Ma with her usual kindly smile, but Pa with visage grim.
One sister to the other cried, 'What can we say to him?'
One of the pair of playboys, noting her father's glower,
Unseen did slip with his fair maid unto leafy bower,
Where both could stay well hidden, and quite concealed from
view,
And hear the sentence being passed upon the other two.
The first to speak was Father, as in rage he crushed a flower:
'Beware of boys who take you up the mountains of the Tower;
Unless you do, you'll surely rue, and pay a heavy price;
Oh daughter, foolish daughter, take a father's good advice.'
Then softly spoke the mother, and to her girl did say:
'Enjoy yourself when you are young, for you'll be old some day;
Enjoy yourselves, be prudent, then I will think no shame;
When I was youthful like yourselves I did the very same.'

3

Looking Around Glenaan and Glendun

The next point of interest in our tour is Glenaan, where, at Lubitavish, is situated 'Ossian's Grave', a stone circle which bears some semblance – though much smaller in size – to 'The Giant's Ring' near Belfast, one of the Stonehenge type of prehistoric monuments.

(Stonehenge, you may remember, is a circular row of large stones, 10,000 feet in circumference, situated on Salisbury Plain, and presented to the nation by Sir Cecil H. Chubb, Bt. It is thought to be the remains of an ancient Druidical temple.)

Glenaan road, famed also for its fuchsia hedges, is situated about a mile north of Cushendall, and a short distance along this road we see a signpost pointing to a hill a quarter-mile away. A loaning leads to a burn, across which stepping stones are arranged, and an easy gradient along a rutted track brings us through the 'street', 'caasay' – or whatever you like to call it – between a farmhouse and its byres, to where a whin-clad slope lies before us. The climb is steeper now, and we are not sorry to pause at a little wayside well to drink, and admire the many varieties of ferns growing in its vicinity; then a few minutes more and we see the 'Grave', set in the middle of a field surrounded by golden whins, whose bloom seems like captured sunshine.

The stones are mostly narrow, set up in a rough circle, with a smaller circle at the western segment, and to the ordinary visitor who has not read any of the learned theories concerning the construction of this monument, or place of Druidical sacrifice, or whatever it may be, it may seem a bit disappointing. Formerly there were plaques, in addition to a noticeboard, which gave the visitor useful information, but these have been removed for some reason.

Returning to the Glenaan road again we questioned some local lads sitting propped against a ditch, but the sphinx or the Wise Old Owl had nothing on these youngsters!

'What happened to the metal plaques used to be up at Ossian's Grave?' we queried.

'Dunno.'

'Is it long since they were removed?'

'Dunno.'

We then tried another method of approach:

'Wasn't the Battle of Aura fought not far from here?'

'A-aye?' – in questioning tone.

'Where is Aura?'

Just a perceptible flicker of two pairs of eyes towards the head of Glenaan, then: 'Up there.'

'Did you ever see where the battle was supposed to have been fought?'

Heads shaken negatively.

'Do you use peats around here?'

'A-aye.'

'Where do you cut?'

A moment's hesitation, then one word showed the quest was hopeless:

'Aura!'

It was the turn of Mr McIlwee and I to shake our heads (at each other) as we mounted our bicycles and rode away, each silently pondering over the interest taken by modern youth in the traditions of its native land!

Ossian, the warrior bard, is said to have been born and reared on Lurigedan, where his father, Finn, was leader of the Fianna. Many beautiful poems are ascribed to him, some of these being in the *Book of Leinster;* but in 1760 a Scot named James Macpherson set out to prove that Ossian was from North of the Tweed — and nearly succeeded!

He published translations of *Fingal and Tremore*, by Ossian and even the cleverest scholars were at first deceived, for Macpherson had undoubtedly great imagination and poetic talent. The first suspicion arose when he was unable to produce the original manuscript, whence he had 'translated', and, later, the general feeling was well-indicated by the following letter from Dr Samuel Johnson (Boswell's *Life*):

Mr James Macpherson,

I received your foolish and impudent letter. Any violence offered me I shall do my best to repel; and what I cannot do for myself the law shall do for me. I hope I shall never be deterred from detecting what I think a cheat by the menaces of a ruffian.

What would you have me retract? I thought your book an imposture; I think it an imposture still. For this opinion I have given my reasons to the public, which I here dare you to refute. Your rage I defy. Your abilities since your Homer, are not formidable; and what I hear of your morals inclines me to pay regard not to what you shall hear, but to what you shall prove. You may print this if you will.

Sam Johnson

Eventually, Ossian's nationality was restored, and in recent years Dr Douglas Hyde dispelled any lingering doubts regarding the authenticity of McPherson's clever forgery.

Fairly late in the last century a visitor with some knowledge of music and keen observation noted that in the less accessible parts of the Glens highlands a few of the songs of Ossian were still sung. Visit those places today and even the persuasive power of Sam Henry (our greatest modern collector of Ulster folk songs) could hardly unearth more than a fragment or two. The introduction of jazz, jitterbug, and their kindred futilities, 'plugged' by radio, has almost killed the taste for our native music, its sole hope for revival resting in the Festivals and Feiseanna which battle to prevent a once musical race from becoming inferior copyists of West African tom-tom artists!

The Battle of Aura

That Battle of Aura, already mentioned, has been a bone of contention among our historians for many years. Some hold that there never was a 'Battle of Aura', while others point to the wealth of circumstantial evidence that has been handed down by local tradition. (Judging by what information was imparted by two Glenaan lads Mr McIlwee and his friend encountered, the handing-down process has now ceased!)

That there was a battle fought on the top of Aura Mountain

seems beyond question, but when we come to the question of what leaders opposed each other there, we come up against stories which do not quite coincide, and even in some cases complete anachronisms are obvious.

Let us take the data available and we may be able to construct a coherent story: It is generally agreed that the McQuillans and McDonnells opposed each other that day, the McQuillans having for allies some of the O'Neills, under Phelim McHugh O'Neill.

Moore ('Dusty Roads', not 'Melodies' Moore) was author of the following verses:

The Battle of Aura

Say, heard you the tidings, now, Donaghy Mor,
Or saw you the signal shine forth from the shore,
Of our kinsmen a thousand hath landed at Torr,
And the standard is raised on the heights of Torcor.
McQuillan, the fierce, on the donagh hath sworn,
Unavenged his fair sister no longer shall mourn;
With lance and with sabre 'mid havoc and flame
To blot from his 'scutheon fair Eveleen's shame.
McDonnell, the haughty, to Aura hath come,
With hauberk, battleaxe, standard and drum,
With message insulting the treacherous knave
Hath dared to the combat McQuillan the brave.

A couple of verses follow, descriptive of the arrival of the clans who are to join McQuillan (you may notice that Moore's poem reflects the general McQuillan sentiment) and then their names are given – McKillop, O'Neill and O'Hara.

As with all battles, comes the aftermath:

For the bravest shall lie in the dawnlight together,
Beneath the blue sky in the depths of the heather,
Unburied and stark in the red fields of slaughter,
Their life-blood encrimsons the dun sullen water.
He fought a hard fight, but he fought it in vain,
McDonnell hath conquered, McQuillan is slain;
Transfixed by a shaft from the hosts of McCaura
He perished that day on the red field of Aura.

The McQuillans

The McQuillans are supposed to have been originally a Norman family, De Mandeville, who were seneschals of the 'Route' (a stretch of land extending from near where Ballymena stands to Portrush, and from the Cloughwater to the Bann).

Deriving their authority from the De Burgos, Earls of Ulster, the virtual disappearance of English authority caused them to mingle more with their neighbours until by adoption of the native customs and language they became McQuillans, Lords of the Route, and clan-neighbours of the McDonnells (whose power was gradually growing greater owing to the influx of their cousins from across the North Channel).

Only two things could have kept such powerful neighbours at peace with one another – either generations of intermarriage or the dire necessity for a long-term alliance against a common enemy.

Strangely enough, it was a combination of a temporary alliance against the O'Cahans (O'Kanes) and a marriage between a McDonnell and a McQuillan that was the indirect cause of the final showdown.

McQuillan had been fighting a riever's feud with O'Kane ('you take my cattle; I take yours') and it happened to be his turn to collect when Colla McDonnell arrived with a small force, on his way to take part in some other 'wee war'.

McQuillan received them at Dunluce, his stronghold, and entertained Colla and his men so well that they felt some slight acknowledgement was due, so they offered their host a day's fighting versus O'Kane.

McQuillan jumped at the offer, and in the subsequent raid the 'redshanks' proved themselves so adept that the combined forces drove home two cows for every one O'Kane had ever 'collected' in a descent upon the Route.

This pleased everybody (except, of course O'Kane) and McQuillan bade his visitors a regretful farewell, bidding them return about Christmas, when there would be more time for entertaining.

Colla accepted the invitation and in due course arrived back at Dunluce, where he and his higher-ranking officers were installed in the Castle, and other clansmen billeted in the McQuillan houses round about.

All went well for a time, but Colla McDonnell was neither dastard in war nor laggard in love, so when he fell in love with Eveleen, Chief McQuillan's daughter, he wasn't long until he had the young lady of the same mind as himself.

This pleased her father all right, but not her brothers, who did not relish the thought of a McDonnell being related to them by any closer tie than friendship.

McDonnell sensed this hostility, and got his inamorata to agree to a secret marriage.

Baffled, McQuillan's sons arranged that at a given signal the Scots should all be attacked and slain, a plan which miscarried only because their sister Eveleen, now Colla's wife, warned her husband in time for him and his men to fly to Rathlin. Here he enlisted some of his kinsmen, returned to the mainland, and superior force made the Clan accept him as the Chief's son-in-law.

Needs must, and the Route men bore it as long as they could, but when Colla died, and they found that Eveleen's Scottish husband had directed that the next in succession was not to be Eveleen's son but Sorley Boy, his own youngest brother, they rebelled and with the help of the Clannagoy O'Neills, defeated Sorley who fled back to Scotland.

Early next year the McQuillans got a message challenging them to meet the McDonnells again, and on the scene of the latter's defeat.

The challenge was, of course, accepted, and another victory made reasonably sure by the addition to the McQuillan army of a powerful force of horse-soldiers under Hugh McPhelim O'Neill. The locals encamped at the head of Glenshesk awaiting their foes who landed at Cushendun and marched to meet them.

One of O'Neill's men, curious about these Scottish highlanders who so persistently were defeated, yet came back for more, asked his Chief for leave to slip down the Glen and have a look at them. This granted, he got within sight of them, and their appearance so impressed him that he hurried back to warn O'Neill that the Glensmen were underestimating their opponents.

O'Neill, proud of his cavalry, and conscious of the fact that foot soldiers were ordinarily no match for horsemen, listened at first good-humouredly, but became incensed by McIlmoyle's insistence, and retorted at last: 'Go join the Scots if you think so much of them!'

Highly offended, McIlmoyle, who had always been a loyal follower of O'Neill, left the camp, went down to meet the McDonnell host and offered to guide them, also betraying the layout of his late master's and McQuillan's forces.

A little suspicious at first, they dissembled until several proofs convinced them of McIlmoyle's transfer of allegiance, whereupon they put him in charge of a portion of their forces and conferred with him regarding the best way to immobilise the cavalry.

Next day was spent in preparation for the struggle, but at night, while the McQuillan host rested, only a few sentries being posted here and there, the Scots busied themselves at digging pits in the boggy ground between their own camp and that of the enemy. These pits they cleverly covered with light branches and heather so that there was no evidence of the night's work. (There you have an example of camouflage!)

Having learnt from McIlmoyle at what part of the camp O'Neill's forces were quartered, the Scots sent a party next morning, all lightly-armed, to taunt and jeer at the horsemen who bore it for a while, then mounted and dashed in pursuit. The McDonnell party appeared to flee in confusion, dashing hither and thither, but in reality they were themselves dodging the pits and leading their enemies into them.

One after another the horsemen floundered in the morass, where they were quickly despatched by the suddenly-rallied Scots. Other parties of the Highlanders converged on the scene, and soon the whole McQuillan encampment was being attacked.

A desperate struggle ensued, in which all the McQuillan leaders were slain except Hugh McPhelim O'Neill. He, badly wounded, and seeing further resistance hopeless, tried to escape on horseback, but could only make as far as Aura Top, where he lay down.

Here he was found by McIlmoyle, to whom he offered a large reward in return of help in escaping, but his former esquire – who seems to have been a thoroughgoing sort of character – told him he would be getting a good reward for that day's work anyway, and killed him!

O'Neill's cairn, called 'Hugh McPhelim's Grave' is still visible on Aura and in Glenshesk there is a 'McQuillan's Grave'.

The day of the McQuillans as a power in North Antrim was ended and henceforth the McDonnells were almost undisputed masters of the Route.

By a patent dated May 10, 1607, James I conferred upon Rory Oge McQuillan the estate of Ballymenagh (Ballymena) which he held until 1618 when he sold it to Sir Faithful Fortescue. Eventually the estate became the property of the Adair family, during the reign of Charles I, and it has remained in their hands ever since.

Romance and the Puzzle of the 'Fuldiew' Stone

Turning left from the foot of Glenaan, a few miles further on we come to where the road forks, one branch leading to Knocknacarry and Cushendun, the other to Glendun and (over the 'Big Bridge') across Carey Mountain to Ballycastle.

Knocknacarry, a lovely little spot nestling at the foot of the mountain, has had a storied past.

It was here that many of the people congregated, during the

time of the Penal persecutions, to carry out the practices of their religion. One of these 'Mass Rocks', which is literally a rock cut in the shape of an altar, was used for many years, Oliver Plunkett having said Mass at it while in hiding in the district.

A short distance away is the little Catholic Church, a reminder that we live in more tolerant times, and the numerous headstones bear the names of people who have played a more prominent part in Ulster life.

Names like McSparran, McAuley, McDonnell and O'Hara occur frequently, but there is one stone (lying flat on the ground not far from the gate as you enter the graveyard) which has puzzled antiquaries for nearly 150 years.

Mrs Craik (1826–87) in her famous novel *John Halifax, Gentleman,* referred to it; the late F.J. Bigger, MRIA, described it in the *Ulster Journal of Archaeology*: Moira O'Neill wrote a story (*Born at Hallowe'en,* published in *Blackwood's Magazine,* December 1890) which was a brave but not wholly satisfactory attempt to account for it, but it was Mr Sam Henry, the well-known folklorist, collector of folk-songs, writer and lecturer, who set himself to solve the puzzle, and succeeded in unearthing the most satisfactory solution yet presented.

The inscription upon the stone reads:

CHARLES Mc
ALASTERS BURR
ING PLACE
HERE LIES THE
BODDY OF JOHN
HIS SON DIED 11
MARCH 1803
AGED 18 YEARS

Below this is a crude drawing of a sailing ship with lengths of cable extending from the bow and stern to anchors, and on the left of the ship, almost level with the truck of the main mast, is a roughly carved representation of something resembling a goat!

This may seem a strange decoration for a tombstone, but the inscription is even more odd:

YOUR SHIP
LOVE IS MOR
ED HEAD AND
STARN FOR A
FULDIEW

Let us examine the local tradition and see if we can make sense of it: John McAlaster (McAllister, we'll call him) was courting a lovely wee lassie from Cushendun, but times weren't too good about home ('love on the dole' wasn't possible then) so he thought he would go to sea and earn enough to set up house.

One day in April, when nature was busy covering the Glen with the green shoots of spring, changing its dun appearance into the glory of the emerald, and birds were trying out their love notes in preparation for mating-time, the lad and his love bade each other a sad farewell, and he started off in search of a ship.

Several weeks elapsed before word came that John had got a berth, then for many long months not a line was received (a not unusual experience in those days!). At last came a letter, bearing the glad tidings that the girl might expect to see her sailor boy shortly, home for a run.

Very welcome, but the best news of all was in the last few

words! These told her to get as many arrangements as possible made for the wedding!

You can imagine the delighted flutter she got into, not a thing ready, dresses to be made, bridesmaids to be selected and asked, 'something old, something new, something borrowed and something blue' to be prepared – and John maybe already on his way home!

It's almost certain that she said to somebody, 'Now isn't that just like a man!'

As soon as possible she set off over the mountain to Glenravel, where she had girl cousins and spent some days in trousseau-making, happy in the thought that her beloved would soon be safe home again.

A couple of days after her departure, a schooner was seen heading in for Cushendun Bay. She came to anchor, a boat was lowered and came towards the beach.

Everybody in the vicinity flocked to the shore to greet the visitor, but the exchange of shouts and banter usual on such occasions fell into a low murmur of speculation as some keener-eyed man spotted a shrouded bundle in the stern-sheets.

Silence fell, broken only by the lapping of the wavelets on the strand and the rattle of the rowlocks as the boat beached.

An officer stepped over the gunwale, and came slowly up the sand to where the silent crowd waited, huddled as crowds will when waiting for news they fear.

'Anyone among you named McAllister?' he asked.

There were many McAllisters present, but none answered save one elderly man, who stepped forward as he had often done in his seafaring days (he had sailed with Nelson when they were both boys and retained his friendship when Nelson became the famous Admiral), saluted and said quietly:

'I am McAllister.'

The officer gave him a look of commiseration, signed to a sailor in the boat, who drew away the canvas.

McAllister looked. 'It is my son,' he said.

The words broke the spell that held the neighbours, who gathered round the boat, lifted the corpse on their shoulders and, in sad procession, escorted it to the bereaved father's home.

The sailors followed and on the way told how, the previous evening, while beating up for Cushendun Bay, where young McAllister was to be put ashore, a fall from aloft had left the young man a broken corpse at the foot of the mainmast!

The interment took place next morning in the family burying-place, and that evening the girl returned from her visit, as yet unaware of what had occurred.

Some neighbours, who themselves had relatives at sea, broke the news as gently and sympathetically as possible, but no burst of tears or other outward manifestation of sorrow showed itself after the one shriek.

She listened with pale, yet composed countenance, then walked unassisted to her room, where for hours she sat silent, gazing out at the sea, the shimmering, now-calm sea, that had deprived her of all she held dearest.

Towards nightfall she slipped quietly from the house but some hours had elapsed before any alarm was felt, as it was thought she had gone to see old McAllister.

When it was found that she was in none of the neighbouring houses, search parties were organised, but the sun was rising out in the east, the lark's clear song was sounding overhead, and the lambs were bleating to their dams, ere they found her dew-soaked form.

She lay, as in an abandonment of grief, across the stone that covered the mortal remains of her lover.

She, too, was dead.

It is surmised that during the hours she spent in the graveyard she must have carved the ship, the animal, and the inscription below them, then when her task was done the weight of her sorrow must have proved too much for her and death mercifully released her spirit to rejoin that of her sailor lad.

The 'fuldiew' part of the inscription could be reconciled with no known expression, though many and ingenious were the theories, until Mr Sam Henry found in old naval records that when a ship was laid up (either for dry-docking or handing over to the ship breakers) the sailors received all leave that had accrued during the voyage, that is, a 'full due'.

This seems a quite reasonable explanation especially when it is remembered that McAllister pere had been in the Navy and she may have heard him use the expression, 'Moored, head and starn, for a full due.'

On the other hand, why did old McAllister not explain the meaning of the inscription if it was so simple?

Career of Ronald McNeill

Ronald McNeill – to give him the name by which his native place best remembers him – was born at Cushendun, his father having at that time Cushendun House but he spent some of his earliest years with his maternal grandmother at Ballycastle. When he was about seven years old his father built a house near Cullybackey, 'Craigdun', which became his home until about 1910.

In that year he returned to Cushendun, repaired 'Glenmona' and made it his home during his holidays or brief spells off from his work at the bar.

After some years as a barrister he entered journalism and in 1900 was made editor of the *St James's Gazette*, also contributing leaders to the *Standard* (later merged with the *Daily Express*). He was one of those who helped to edit the eleventh edition of the *Encyclopaedia Britannica*, his contribution being about one hundred and fifty articles of a biographical or historical nature. Always interested in politics he forsook journalism and tried to enter Parliament as member for West Aberdeenshire, in 1906. He was defeated, as also in Aberdeen City, where he fought the bye-election consequent upon Mr Bryce being appointed Ambassador to Washington.

Again, he tried Aberdeen South, this time in 1910, but it was not until he was elected unopposed for the St Augustine division of Kent that he entered parliament. From 1911 until 1918 he represented St Augustine, but a change in the constituencies in Kent caused Canterbury to be included and he represented this district until 1927.

In 1922 he became Under-Secretary for Foreign Affairs, but the change to a Labour Government in 1923 drove him from office. In 1925, however, he returned to the Cabinet as Financial Secretary to the Treasury. Created Lord Cushendun in 1927, he reached full Cabinet rank as Chancellor of the Duchy of Lancaster and represented Britain at the League of Nations at Geneva.

On Friday, October 12, 1934 he died, deeply regretted not only by his immediate relatives and fellow-statesmen, but also by the plain folk of his native Glens, people who will recall the kindly acts of Ronald McNeill when the achievements of Lord Cushendun may be relegated to a few lines in history books.

The Gallery of Glendun

When one first approaches Glendun, there is a distinct semblance to a glen in the Scottish Highlands. The tree-clad slopes with patches of cultivated land peeping through, and above them the heather-covered mountain-top, combine to form a picture reminiscent of somewhere in Argyllshire, the only thing missing being the waters of the loch.

Glendun folk are proud of their 'Big Bridge', a viaduct which spans the river and links the roads on each side of the glen. On the northern side is the route to Carey and Ballycastle but our way lies more to the left, where we enter a 'loaneen' — as it is called in the musical local dialect — that winds across the face of the hillside.

Short though the distance is from where modern traffic in the form of cars and lorries speeds along, up here the people utilise only wheel-car or slipe as a method of transport. Lovers of the picturesque can obtain some good photographs of these quaint vehicles in action but let no visitor imagine that the slipes are completely outmoded affairs! On the precipitous slopes of all the Glens they serve a purpose for which no satisfactory substitute has yet been evolved.

Watch one of them as the sure-footed little pony or donkey negotiates a mountain path whose surface is strewn with debris from the overhanging cliffs, stones of all sizes and shapes, ranging from 'kidney-stones' to boulders the size of a man's head. How skilfully the animal draws its load of turf, using its hoofs as brakes, and at times sliding on its haunches down a particularly steep place, and how cannily the soft-wood 'feet' grip or slither over the rugged surfaces they encounter!

We have already seen how the Cushendall pony is being

allowed to die out, but no better case for its survival could be offered than to show one of these cat-footed animals in action between the shafts of a slipe or a wheel-car.

The slipe or wheel-car consists of two shafts, the after ends resting upon the two feet or 'slipes' (sloping pieces of wood acting as do the runners of a sleigh). Across the shafts are two strong battens, about four feet apart, and on the top of these rests the 'creel' for holding whatever is carried. In later developments the wicker-work was superseded by wooden slats, but the initial shape remained the same, sloping slightly backward (so as to maintain the load in an almost horizontal position on the downgrades).

The slopes of Glendun are inhabited by people whose descent from the Scots can easily be traced, and many of whose relations today are living in Glasgow or the West of Scotland.

They are very kindly people, like the most of hill-dwellers, and proud. There have been occasional visitors who have adopted a patronising attitude, but have rather ungently come back to earth upon discovering that many Glendun people can prove relationship with, or descent from, some of the most famous names in Scottish or Irish history!

'Gold in Ballyteerim'

Like the Ballyteerim woman's reaction when she read Moira O'Neill's line quoted: 'All the gold in Ballyteerim is what's sticking to the whins.'

'Heth!' says she, 'She needn't be sayeen that about us! When the Hickiesons (Higginson, Moira O'Neill's family name) were about Cushendun there's plenty of us had as much gold as they had!'

There are plenty of McNeills, McAllisters and O'Haras in Glendun, and McAuleys, descendants of the McAuley clansmen who were a deciding factor in the winning of the Battle of Aura. There is the McNeill home on Erragh Tops where Sam Henry, MRSAI, and I partook of the turkey egg, the while the woman o' the house sang for us some old songs that even Sam, a life-long collector of folk songs, had never heard before.

Up here, too, on 'the Gallery of Glendun', is where the road suddenly ends at nowhere in particular and for no visible reason. Enquiry elicited an explanation:

Many years ago there was a man who had many daughters, their only dowry, besides their good looks, being their housewifery. In open competition with lassies whose dowry lay in more material things his girls had a poor chance, so mercenary-minded were the local swains, and after much thought Father evolved a plan.

He built a house up here, with no road or loaning leading directly to it, knowing – wise old psychologist that he was – that curiosity is by no means confined to the fair sex!

His plan worked.

Young men, out on a Sunday or holiday evening to see what they could see, couldn't see why a house should be so isolated, and called to see why.

Once the spider had got the flies into the parlour, and they saw so many sweet things there, his work was done, and the artless (?) wiles of his daughters spun another web around them from which they had no desire to escape.

He got his daughters married, then left the house, and for years after it was tenantless – wherein lies a moral, maybe!

Glendun, the Brown Glen

Glendun means the 'Brown Glen', but this is nowadays only true of Glendun in late autumn when the last leaves are fallen from the trees, the fronds of the bracken are withered, the heather is turned a dull russet and the little river is full of brown water.

In spring Glendun is a green glen where the soft blades of grass, the little shoots of larch-needles and the odd speckles of early whin-blossom or the primrose contrast with the redness of ploughland.

In summer Glendun is a feast of beauty, a painter's heartbreak, where the colours in his kit seem too few to depict the varying tints that must be captured on canvas if his picture is to be worthwhile.

Winter sends Glendun into a state of somnolence, a drowsy quiet which extends to everything but the river. Then what was a little gurgling, laughing stream becomes a foaming torrent, as if, in the quiet glen, it shouted, 'But I go on forever!' There are, of course, winter nights when the wind howls eerily round the houses, when the whipping of the tortured larches sounds even above the wind that causes it, but such things do not trouble the people of the glens who sit cosily around their blazing turf fires and while the ceilidh hours away with cheerful chat, joke, music and dance.

The Plantation

There are several roads leading into or away from Glendun. One, the mountain road, winds in leisurely fashion up over the top of Aura, and meets the Ballycastle route near Newtowncrommelin, passing a spot where a settlement or 'Little Plantation' was attempted by Nicholas Delacherous Crommelin over a hundred years ago. This Crommelin was a descendant of Louis Crommelin, a Huguenot who took shelter here from religious persecution in France and who founded the Ulster linen industry.

The 'Plantation' was a failure as the land was so poor that the scanty crops would not support the settlers and in winter the weather was so bad that instead of 'Skerry Ravel' they called the place 'scare the devil!'

There was a ballad used to be sung in the Glenravel district of which the following is a typical extract:

> Where moorfowl were plenty
> And hares made their den,
> 'Twas a wild habitation
> For Crom'lin's white men.

Nicholas Crommelin was also the first to attempt to work the ore that lay – untold millions of tons of it – a few feet below the surface of all the land from Glenarm to Glenariff, and from Templepatrick to Glenravel.

Although in this attempt he was also unsuccessful, credit must be given to him for having directed attention to the existence of this potential wealth.

Some years later, Father Macaulay, the then Parish Priest of Glenravel, tried to interest Mr Fisher (an English visitor on holiday at Cleggan, Braid district) in the ore.

Fisher, who hailed from Barrow-in-Furness, the iron and steel manufacturing port in Lancashire, was at first a bit doubtful whether the quantity – and quality – of ore obtained would make it a paying proposition. Father Macaulay, to set his doubts at rest, got a man who had years of experience as a miner in Scotland,

Mr William McQuitty, to open up several seams and obtain samples.

The Iron-Ore Mines

McQuitty did so, and his report, backed by the samples of rich ore, converted Fisher so thoroughly that he enthusiastically threw himself into the task of opening mines, building rows of cottages (bothies, the imported Scottish miners called them) and laying railway lines to convey the ore from Slievenanee, Evishnacrow and other mines to the nearest port, whence his ships carried it across to the furnaces of Millom, Duddon, Maryport and Whitehaven.

Another company, the Glenariff Iron Ore and Harbour Company, was started in Glenariff, and for many years it also shipped ore (via its own pier at what is today called the 'White Arch' near the Catholic Chapel) to the Cumberland ports.

The full story of how such a promising industry was allowed to go to ruin has never fully been told – and this is not the time to tell it – but the few survivors of that heyday of coastal Antrim speak of it as a time of unparalleled prosperity, when it seemed as if this poor-soiled district was about to become one of the richest in all Ireland.

During the 1939-45 war, hopes were revived when the scarcity of metals, particularly aluminium, became acute (Glenariff ore contains an average of thirty per cent alumina) but for some reason – or none – the ore was allowed to lie there, like some great treasure awaiting a magician's wand, while iron gates and aluminium saucepans were being melted down.

Five hundred million pounds (£500,000,000) were spent in developing the famous atomic bomb, or in knocking a chip off the mighty atom, but no money has ever been forthcoming to develop this natural wealth that might have made our country prosperous.

Section and Analysis of Metallic Ores near Glenarm, Co. Antrim

Main ore bed average 3 ft in thickness, Lithomarge 20–100 feet.

+ Pisolithic iron ore – 2 feet; 36 per cent metallic iron (Geo. Survey, 1912: analysis of ores mined showed 60 per cent iron in some cases), 27 per cent alumina – 7.20 cwts iron per ton.
+ Pavement – 2 feet; 27 per cent metallic iron, 30 per cent alumina – 5.40 cwts iron per ton.
+ Pavement – 2 feet; 25 per cent metallic iron, 30 per cent alumina – 5 cwts iron per ton.
+ Pavement – 2 feet; 22 per cent metallic iron, 34 per cent alumina – 3.4 cwts iron per ton.
+ Lithomarge – 20 feet; 17 per cent metallic iron, 40 per cent alumina – 3.4 cwts iron per ton.

The mining engineer whose tables are quoted was engaged in a consultative capacity upon projects such as one costing $3,000,000 in the Ukraine and others connected with mine mechanisation in the USA.

Glenravel, while it was the centre of the ore industry, possessed a flourishing distillery situated near Cargan, or 'Fisherstown' as it was called for a while in compliment to the mine-owner. This distillery (not to be thought of as a 'poteen' manufactory, I hope!) had a short but very lucrative existence, though today little remains of the building in which 'Glenravel Whiskey' was manufactured.

Cargan Lammas Fair, an annual event which at one time promised to outdo the famous Ballycastle 'Oul' Lammas Fair', faded when Glenravel's prosperity declined, and today the only throb that disturbs the peace of this curlew-haunted spot is when the shepherds, dealers, dogs and sheep – plus the auctioneer – gather for the annual sheep sale, where anything from 5,000 to 7,000 ewes, rams, wethers and lambs are disposed of.

We have strayed into Glenravel, which is not one of the famous Nine Glens, so we'd better get back to the coast again. As the French saying has it 'Revenons à nos moutons' – so we'll return to our subject by following the road leading over past Cregagh Planting through a sheep-dotted, heather-clad mountain, then down between embankment past a quarry and so to the dark lough of Carey ('Loughareema') near Glendun.

The Lough where a Coach sank

This lough is almost dry in summer (that is, a real summer, not the rainy season that we had for summer in late years!), but in winter it becomes a fairly respectably-sized lake, which makes the road impassable. This was the scene of a tragedy many years ago when a Colonel McNeill and his coachman were drowned one dark night.

Driving two spirited horses, the coachman did not notice that the road was now in the bed of the lake, and, before he could draw up the coach, horses and men were well into the deep brown water.

Their bodies were found a couple of days later.

Moira O'Neill's poem has been so often quoted that any reference to Loughareema seems incomplete without it, so while we are beside the dark lough we'll listen to her description:

Loughareema! Loughareema!
Lies so high among the heather.
A little lough, a dark lough,
The waters black and deep.
Ould herons go a-fishing there,
And seagulls all together
Float round the one green island
On the fairy lough asleep.

Even before Col. McNeill and his man met their death there, Loughareema had a dark reputation: 'The Lord between us and harm! But it was a wild place to be benighted.' Any Glensman would have made a detour which entailed an addition to his journey of four or five miles, or would leave a bit of business unfinished, rather than be in the vicinity of the lough after nightfall.

Its name, of which 'the Lough of the Fairies' is a very free translation, was enough to keep believers in the 'wee people' from visiting it, particularly at 'fairy' times such as Hallowe'en, Christmas or St John's Eve.

It was said that 'an unholy sprite' – as Moore described her in his poem *The Lord of Dunluce* – haunted the spot, a being something like the kelpie of the Scottish lochs, but other tales described the doings of fairy folk who did not seem to have any ill-feeling towards travellers who unwittingly invaded the spot.

I have been told of the experience of several quarrymen who, almost fifty years ago, were staying in a traction engine van which was parked close to the loughside.

Night after night, when they were in bed, these men were awakened by the noise of many wee voices chattering near the

111

van. Listening more intently, they could just make out the noise of music, apparently at some distance, but as soon as any of them went to the door to investigate, a dead silence fell and the sound did not start again until they had returned to bed!

Over twenty years ago I stayed for a fortnight in a house situated about a mile on the Cregagh side of Carey Lough, and though I saw no fairies I certainly did feel that if there are any of the 'Good People' left, then Loughareema would be an ideal spot for them. There is an air of enchantment, a queer long-ago look about the place as if time had stood still there and at any moment kilted clansmen might rise from the heather and join with men in lowland dress in a stern struggle, flashing claymore clashing with broadsword, with red-faced, red-shanked pipers playing wild tunes to stimulate the martial ardour of the mountaineers.

Not so very imaginative, either, for almost every foot of land about here has been fought over by the McDonnells during their long struggle to establish their supremacy in North Antrim.

Journey in the Old Days

We have yet to get to the more northern glens, Glencorp, Glenshesk and Glentaisi, but let us first have a retrospective view of the road that rounded the shores of Antrim prior to the construction of the now-famous Coast Road.

(We are back in the year 1810; Napoleon has recently divorced Josephine Beauharnais, and his armies are predominant on the European continent; George III, bluff old 'Farmer George', is on the throne of England.)

The coach in which we are travelling has just left Larne behind, and is taking its leisurely but noisy way over the deeply-rutted track that winds along the hillside from Larne.

Now and then the coachman sounds a note or two on his horn, this both for the purpose of announcing the coming of the 'stage' to intending passengers (no limited stops operate) and acting as a warning to other road users, including the hens, dogs, pigs, sheep or cattle that this modern juggernaut might frighten if it arrived unheralded!

Just how bad the road can be is shown by the subject now being discussed by the 'inside' passengers – the bogging of another coach a week ago, when a wheel came off, the coachman was injured and it took two days of hard work to get the vehicle back to Larne for repairs.

In 1841, over thirty years later, when Mr and Mrs S.C. Hall visited Glenarm, they asked an old man how the coach-and-six of an earlier date had managed to negotiate such a road. His reply was:

'Och, this was the way of it,' he said, 'first and foremost we tuck the horses off, and then the beasts got on well enough when they had nothing heavier than themselves to drag; then the quality got out and walked, and a power o' men turned up from the glens and drew the carriage. Oh, bedad! We managed it bravely.'

Well, the descent – or, as the Glensman said, the climb down – into Glenarm is by way of that same road, and the coachman skilfully uses his horn to wake up the sleepy village, then the horses are brought to a stop that almost sends them on their haunches.

Ostlers dash out, unhook the traces, and lead the steaming nags to the stables, while mine host with rubicund visage takes his place on the inn steps to welcome the passengers. The coachman descends in a rotundity due to many overcoats, and in leisurely fashion waddles to the tap-room, there to imbibe some liquid 'cheer' and regale the open-mouthed villagers with tales of the perils of the road.

Some of the passengers elect to put up at the inn, despite the statement of R. Dobbs a hundred or so years before that 'Glenarm afforded only ill-lodging and bad cooks'! So we leave them when the fresh team is yoked.

We are driven over the bridge near Glenarm Castle and, climbing over Straidkilly, see Glencloy and Carnlough. Through Carnlough we go at a spanking pace, then up past Limnalary House, the residence of Peter Mathewson, Esq., Captain of the Glenarm Yeomanry (and destined later on to be the home of a more famous soldier, Field-Marshal Sir George Stuart White, VC, GCB, OM, GCMG, GCIO, GCVO, the hero of Ladysmith).

The going here is better, as the new owner of the Drumnasole estate, a Mr Francis Turnley, has since his coming to the district employed men in improving the surface of the road leading to where he has erected a large residence which is known as Drumnasole House.

Local gossip says that Mr Turnley spent some years in China, where he amassed a fortune of £80,000, then returned home and bought Cushendall and Drumnasole.

We pass a roadside well that somebody says is called 'Tubberdoney', whose water has a great reputation in the locality for the treatment of affections of the eyes; then a little schoolhouse comes to view, and some way above it the partly-finished mansion of larch and fir trees extending from near it right up to the brow of the mountain.

A lovely drive takes us over two humped-backed bridges, then past Nappan, where resides John Higginson, Esq., Major of the Antrim Militia (and ancestor of Moira O'Neill, poetess, of *Songs of the Glens of Antrim* fame).

From Nappan our pace increases and soon we are passing Garron Head, crowned by Dunmaul, an ancient stronghold ringed by a fosse; then we descend to a point near the sea, crossing a rivulet (Foran) that springs from the face of the limestone rock.

A depression close to the shore is pointed out as 'St Patrick's Heel', where the saint is supposed to have put his foot down when crushing the serpents that were reluctant to enter the sea when he banished them.

There is little more than a track from this point up to Galbolly, so we have to walk while the sweating horses strain and pull the coach up to the village. There is a dark, withdrawn look about it that is not inviting, and the inhabitants – or the few we see – do not appear to be very hospitable. (We remember, too, that not a lifetime before the place had a reputation for brigandage.)

Re-entering the coach, we drive gaily past Falavee, its white cliffs shining in the rosy light of the setting sun, and as the twilight settles down we pass the ruins of Ardclinis, a monastery dating back to the thirteenth century.

Glenariff is now is sight, and we slow down passing Milltown, smallest townland in Ireland, which consists of a corn mill, flax mill and clachan of small, neat, whitewashed cottages. Nearby is Bay Lodge, the residence of Rev. Stewart Dobbs, who built the mills referred to and who is a very popular landlord. He has always taken a practical interest in the welfare of his tenantry, though the majority of them do not belong to his church, and has lately (1809) sent a very complete account of their history, mode of life and any interesting topographical features to Mr Mason, editor of the (published 1812) *Statistical Survey of Ireland.* The landlord who succeeded Rev. Dobbs evicted many of the people, and the mills were left derelict. The ruins may still be seen.

Our next stop is, of course, at the cave-home of Nannie Murray, where, while we refresh ourselves with a drop of her special distillation, we are told the story of how she came to be allowed to dispense 'mountain dew' with impunity.

It appears that the then Earl of Antrim heard of Nannie's activities and came to visit her. Upon arrival at her 'premises' he was told – not by Nannie, but by some of her neighbours – of the number of apparently-drowned persons she had restored, and the number of benighted or exhausted travellers to whom she had extended her hospitality. So struck was his Lordship by this evidence of the usefulness of Nannie's service that he obtained permission for her to carry on her good work without the formality of paying rent or licence.

We look upon our hostess with a certain amount of respect, as the only unlicensed retailer of alcoholic beverages permitted to exercise her 'calling' without fear of legal interference, then bid her farewell, and after a steep climb up Crookanavick come in sight of Cushendall.

The horses seem to know they have only a short distance to go and set a spanking pace for the descent into the village where, passing on our left the 'Curfew Tower', a square, sandstone-built building, we come to a stop at the large inn which Mr Turnley has built for the convenience of travellers (Glens of Antrim Hotel) – and journey's end.

Making the Coast Road

The foregoing is a description of the average trip from Larne to Cushendall as it might have been written early in the 1800s, but the genius of Lanyon devised a method of overcoming all obstacle, in the construction of what is now the Antrim Coast Road, a highway – most of it within a biscuit's toss of the sea – which is unsurpassed in Europe.

The obstacles are legion. Rocks had to be blasted, the sea had to be restrained from washing the newly-made road away, the overhanging cliffs in places had to be quarried back far enough to make the passage below them safe and, where other methods failed, the road had to be built away from the cliffs on land reclaimed from the sea itself!

A short description of the general procedure should be of interest. In the first place, a strong foundation was laid, this being effected by blasting pieces of the cliffs away, then utilising the huge boulders thus obtained as a bottom. Over this was spread layer after layer of stones, each layer of smaller-sized pieces than the last, until the required height above high-water level was obtained.

You know the sloping surface that surrounds the base of a sea-girt lighthouse? Well, the base of the road was given a slope after the same principle, a 'battery' it was called, and that battery has withstood the gales and heavy seas of a century without more than one or two small breaches each winter.

John Loudon McAdam (1756-1836), the Scottish engineer who invented the process of road-surfacing that bears his name, had his method adopted in laying our Coast Road, and it was macadamised (later tar-macadamised), until some stretches of it, notably Cushendall – Waterfoot, were asphalted a few years ago.

The only danger encountered by constant users of the Coast Road is from falling rocks. In winter the rain gathers in crevices in the cliffs, and lies there until the frost widens these crevices, then at the thaw portions of rock are dislodged and may start a miniature avalanche.

Several of these falls have been rather serious as, for instance, that at Garronpoint in 1911 or 1912 when hundreds of tons of rock fell on the road and completely blocked it.

(By the way, the writer remembers seeing 'Poet McKie' coming hurriedly from his house just below Dunmaul. No wonder! A huge boulder weighing at least a ton had rolled down the hillside, bounced up on to the roof of the cottage, and was now reposing in the ruins of his bed in the 'room'!)

It has been suggested that to minimise or perhaps completely remove this danger a careful survey should be made of all cliff-faces adjacent to the road and the necessary steps taken to blast away or quarry any of the loose or out-jutting pieces.

Ghost stories usually attach themselves to ancient places and the Coast Road isn't so very ancient, yet it has a ghost story or two concerning certain stretches of it.

The 'White Girl' Ghost

One, the experience of a Glenaan man, tells about one night he was coming from Carnlough driving a horse and cart-load of lime.

At Nappan (about a mile south of Garronpoint) his horse stopped and refused to go any further. Going to its head, he tried to lead it, to no purpose, and was looking around for the cause of the stoppage when - 'Wheee-e-e-e!' a white figure flew with

118

incredible speed from the shore, crossed in front of him, then returned from the hazel wood into which it had disappeared and stood in the middle of the road.

Half-paralysed with fright, he saw that it was the figure of a young woman, all in white, with a queer unearthly light emanating from her face!

She spoke not – he couldn't! – but after a few moments, with the courage of desperation, he pulled the bag he had over his shoulder and covered the horse's head. He then got it induced to advance a few paces, but the instant it passed where the figure stood it whinnied, then set off at a gallop, nor could he pull it up until it reached Falavee, almost three miles away!

Imagination! Hallucination, bad booze or any explanation you like to give is discounted by the fact that numerous other persons, usually sober and level-headed, have declared that they saw this wraith – or whatever it may be. In one case the spectator was unaware of the previous reputation of the spot, yet his description tallied with that of all the others.

So much for the White Girl of Nappan.

The 'Black Gate' Ghost

Garron Tower is supposed to be haunted by the ghost of a butler who should have lost interest in human affairs after almost decapitating himself while severing his carotid arteries with a carving knife. This sanguinary gentleman's gentleman is seen occasionally bearing a basin containing his grinning countenance and surrounds, and it is a certainty that the appearance of a headless torso in such circumstances would have shaken even the most hardened sans-culotte!

Judge, then, of the shock received by a local farmer's

daughter returning home one night, when she saw the Tower butler standing at the Black Gate, Nappan (a mile from his usual haunting-ground).

Naturally enough, she quickened her pace a trifle once she got past him and did a gentle faint when she reached home, but nobody has yet fathomed why he was there, unless, as one wiseacre suggested, that was his night out!

'Bewitched' Mo-bikes!

A short distance from Falavee and almost below Corgradh, Galbolly, is a little rise in the road known as Gillian's Hill.

Some years ago, two motorcyclists from Belfast, down at Waterfoot for the weekend, started on Sunday evening to ride home again. All went well until the leading chap reached Gillian's Hill where his machine suddenly and most unaccountably conked out. He had no sooner stopped than his chum, who had been some distance behind, came along and drew up beside him. They both examined the machine, but could find nothing wrong, so cyclist No. 2 said he would go on to Carnlough and get a mechanic he knew back with him on his pillion.

He tried to start his motorbike, but not a start would she do! This was most annoying, so both of them used all their considerable knowledge of mo-bikes to set the machine going again.

While working thus, one of them happened to turn the front wheel in the direction of Waterfoot — an instantly the engine spluttered into life!

They headed it back towards Carnlough — and instantly it stopped!

'We'll just have to push them back to Waterfoot,' said one,

and his chum agreed.

They somewhat morosely headed their unwieldy machines for Red Bay and had pushed a hundred yards or so when the first to have engine trouble stopped, gave his starting pedal a kick and off she went, ticking over beautifully. No. 2 then tried his, with the same result, and with lighter hearts they headed back for Belfast.

When they reached the exact spot where their machines had refused before, the same thing happened, only that it was No. 2 that was first this time.

They tried three times, then went and stayed at Waterfoot until Monday morning when they rode home without incident.

What complicates matters is the fact that where the queer incident happened has been known as a haunted spot for the past 70 or 80 years!

Fairies at Night School

From ghosts to fairies may – or may not – seem a logical step, but we are on the subject of the Coast Road and there are several fairy tales associated with it (in addition to the one about the fairy birth at Straidkilly, already related). We'll have a look at a typical yarn.

For instance, the little school at Garronpoint, sitting a few yards from the road, had at one time the reputation of being haunted – not by ghosts, but fairies!

An old resident in the vicinity told this story of a queer experience he had: one winter evening over fifty years ago, just as darkness was falling, he happened to be passing the school on his way home from collecting driftwood on the shore.

Light flickering inside the building drew his attention and, fearing that too large a fire had been left behind by the teacher, he opened the gate, went up to the nearest window and looked in.

The fire was certainly burning brightly enough, but what interested him much more was the bunch of about a dozen wee men seated around the hearth, while slowly turning on a spit before the fire was a nice plump chicken!

The sight, though certainly most unusual, wasn't exactly frightening, so he stood for a minute or two in amazement, trying to make up his mind what to do.

At last he gave the window a tap and instantly cries broke from the wee people, water seemed to be thrown on the fire, which was instantly quenched, and complete silence fell!

The narrator told me that the silence seemed to be threatening, and for the life of him he couldn't have stayed there any longer, so took to his heels and told nobody what had occurred.

Next day, when some of the children returned from school, they mentioned how angry the teacher had been at finding the school fire quenched with water, some of which had run over the floor! (In those days the scholars brought peats to supply the fire which usually had a 'gleed' left in it to smoulder and start next morning's blaze.)

Gigs and Boat-race Bards

When we reach Ballycastle in our tour we can learn more about its Lammas Fair, but meanwhile it wouldn't do to leave Glenarm, Carnlough, Cushendall and Cushendun without mentioning the regattas in which their oarsmen have engaged with such keen competition during the past 80 years or so.

Dan McGonnell, 'Butcher Bard of Lurigedan', followed the regattas all round the Antrim Coast, and composed ballads in which he mentioned the stars of the sport.

'Glenarm Regatta' was one of the outstanding events of the year, being the one at which the rivalries of the gig-pulling season were finally settled.

Rowers from Larne, Ballygally, Glenarm, Carnlough, The Largy, Waterfoot, Cushendall, Cushendun and Ballycastle were entered and the scene was one of great excitement as the starting-gun sounded on the 'Committee Boat'.

Away swept the gigs, the cheers and shouts of encouragement their partisans uttered rising to a deafening crescendo s one after another – or sometimes in a bunch – they rounded the turning buoy and strained every nerve and sinew in the ding-dong struggle to the finishing 'post' at the Committee Boat. Listen in: Come on, *Latharna*! Pull! Pull! *Lady Jean*! The *Twilight's* ahead – no, she's not! – She is! There's the *Laurel* overhauling her! The *Laurel's* past her! There's the *O'Halloran* overtaking – The *Glensman's* lying close up! – She's pulling well – The *Laurel's* first turned the buoy – That one behind her is the *Glens Girl* – somebody's bumped – It's the *Lady Jean* and *O'Halloran* – no, lend me your glasses a minute – It's the *Latharna* and the *Twilight* – They're all clear and starting to pull again – They're together, look! They're overhauling the leaders – Good old *Twilight* – well pulled *Latharna* – The *Glensman* is right behind them – The *Glensman's* level! *Glensman* – *Latharna* – *Twilight*! – *Twilight* wins!

And amid the plaudits of both winners and good losets the winning gig turns in for the shore where the victorious if breathless rowers and the cool little coxswain are hoisted on the shoulders of their friends and borne in triumph through the village.

Some of the names of the old-time boats have been perpetuated – the *Glensman*, *Laurel* and *Lady Jean*, *Olderfleet* and *Glens Girl* – though other once-famous names like *Peg Doran*, *Cairn Maid*, *Maid O' the Mill*, *Paddy-Go-Easy* and *Thomas Moore* have gone and only the tradition of their achievement remains.

Tragedy attended one regatta, held at Cushendall many years ago. Three competitors named Montgomery, Bamford and Ellis were drowned when the boat capsized. 'Poet McKie', in a ballad still sung in the Nine Glens, recorded the sad happening. It is called *Montgomery* and begins:

Ye natives of the Antrim Coast, your kind attention pay
While I relate the doleful news we've got in Carnlough Bay
There's many an eye in Carnlough town will fill when this they
   see
That in the silent bottom lies my friend Montgomery.

Racing a Holed Gig
In the first race ever rowed by a Cushendall-owned gig she was victorious and she continued in the same season her winning progress at Ballygally and against a picked crew of coloured seamen at Belfast.

Dan McGonnell immortalised this in a poem of which the following is an extract:

   Long life to bold Jack Beston
   That pulled the stroke so true,
   And likewise Hugh Delargy

And next on Archie Murray
Did all the rest depend,
A gallant crew that pulled us through
In the *Lily of the Glens*.

At a regatta held in Red Bay or Cushendall a competing boat was bumped and holed badly. One of the rowers (the Archie Murray referred to above)took off his hat, rammed it into the hole, held it there with one foot and besought his fellow rowers to continue the race.

They did so and – believe it or not – they won!

Another story concerns a Cushendall crew who (in the *Lily of the Glens*) challenged the best that Glenarm or Carnlough could produce.

The local bank manager, a former Bannside oarsman, volunteered to train them and on the big day took an oar himself.

Rivalry was intense among the partisans of the different boats, and quite a few coats came off – though there were no actual scraps – before they lined up.

The gun! Off they shot and never in the whole long history of gig-racing on the Antrim Coast was a more thrilling struggle witnessed! There was hardly more than a few inches separating their bows as they rounded the buoy, and on the straight for home almost half was covered before superior training began to tell.

The Cushendall boat was the first to emerge from the ruck, then slowly but surely she drew away with another striving hard to close up with her.

On the shore, strong men's voices broke to a childish treble as they yelled themselves hoarse, and women danced up and down like people possessed when the Cushendall gig shot past the committee boat a length in front of its nearest rival!

Bloody; but unbeaten!

A great finish to a great race and as the *Lily of the Glens* came smartly in to the beach people ran into the water almost waist deep to lift the victors out of the gig and carry them shoulder-high ashore.

When the Bannsider bankman's turn came it was seen that where he had sat was covered with blood (an oarsman must be tough!) but all he said was, 'It was worth it all!'

This is only a sample of the scenes when gig-racing was in its heyday, and today an octogenarian's eyes will light up, his voice will take on a firmer note and even a spring comes to his step as he recalls his own or other gig-puller's achievements.

4

Country Crafts and Dialect

A picturesque feature of our rural landscape was once the snug, whitewashed, farm cottage nestling warmly through the wildest winter under its thick coat of thatch. A thatcher was seldom idle, his only slack period being when high wind, snow or a very heavy rain held up the job.

During such periods he usually worked as a basket maker or creel-maker until more clement weather returned.

Thatching was a highly-specialised craft and good thatchers were in great demand, people who took pride in the neatness and weatherproof quality of their roofs paying good prices for the work.

Today the comfortable thatched roof is disappearing. In Glenariff, for example, almost every farmhouse in the glen had a thatched roof — today there only about ten left.

A well-constructed roof of thatch was a pretty sight and had the additional advantages of being warm in winter and cool in summer. As one old man explained to me, 'Gin ye had a good fire on a winter' nicht the thatch aye kep the hate [heat] in, but on a warm summer's day the sun cudnae mak' its way through it.'

The tools used in thatching were a sharp knife, a 'spurtle' (wooden gadget shaped like a catapult stick) and a wooden rake. A new thatch was begun by laying scraws (sods about two feet broad by four feet long) grass-side out on top of wattles which crossed the 'ribs'. The average 'spar' of thatch was about 18 inches, 2 feet in breadth, and consisted of rye or wheat straw – rye for preference, though even rushes or 'bent' (fiorin) grass were used sometimes. The spars were held in position by 'scobes', 'scallops' and 'clasps', work commencing from the 'easing' (wall-top) and finishing at the 'rigging' (where slated roofs have the ridge tile).

In the old days nearly every farmhouse had its spinning wheel or wheels, where the womenfolk spun the wool their men had shorn from the sheep. After being carefully carded, it was spun, then reeled and sent to the weaver, who returned it woven into a blanket which bore more resemblance to a quilt.

Blanket Thickening

The next event in its career was a 'thickening'. Twenty or thirty young men and women of the district were invited to a thickening at which were collected any blankets recently delivered by the weaver. A rod creel was set up in the kitchen, a blanket was well soaped and, standing at opposite sides of the creel, boys and girls pulled it back and forward until it became fluffy and soft, 'the quare man for a cowl night', and thickened until it was about three times as bulky as before the treatment.

It wasn't all work, as there was usually a fiddler present, and the time passed merrily in exchange of jest and song, culminating in an hour of dancing before the party broke up.

'Quilting' was another communal sort of job when a number of women collected at a neighbour's house to sew together the patches of which the quilt was to be made. Pride in neatness and quickness (with the emphasis upon neatness) was a feature of these gatherings, and, though the custom has long died out, many products of these needlewomen are still in use.

As regards women who spin, there is but one left in the whole Nine Glens. The only young person whom I know to be capable of handling the spinning wheel is Miss Margaret Leach of Glenariff, who has carried on the old tradition as a hobby since her mother died, leaving her the wheel. It is difficult nowadays to get cards (for carding, or straightening out the strands prior to spinning) as these have to be obtained from either Donegal or the Scottish Hebrides.

There were at one time so many spinning wheels in use that special tradesmen called wheelwrights were constantly employed in the repair and renewal of them, though strangely enough it was left to old itinerant craftswomen to supply the cards. These cards, made of a piece of wood about 6 inches wide and 8 inches long tapering to a handle, were studded with wire spikes like a curry comb, and special dexterity was required in their use.

The Old Spinning Wheel

A spinning wheel was a simple but ingenious device. It consisted of a wheel about two feet in diameter, 'pins' on which the thread was wound, and was adjustable by means of what was called a 'temper pin'.

Many a time I watched the spinner at work, her hands moving deftly as she added the 'rowans' to the end of the wool being spun, the wheel giving a musical click which contrasted with the chirping of the crickets on the heart, and the peat fire flickering and throwing a dim light in keeping with the task.

Spinning did not require much more concentration than does knitting, and while the wheel busily revolved the spinner could engage in conversation with the others in the kitchen, or listen to the music of the ceilidhers. Most of the spinning was done during the 'fore-supper', when other household tasks were finished.

The materials produced by the home, spinner, weaver – and knitter also – were made of pure wool, and meant to last. The dyes used were mostly derived from local plants, though logwood was also popular, and it is quite likely that a few of the garments of those days would even yet be unearthed from a moth-proof chest or two, their colours as fresh as the day they were packed away.

Old Trades and Industries

Farming has always been the premier industry in the Nine Glens. It was regarded as a sort of hereditary occupation to which many were called but few were chosen! The system was roughly this: a man who had a good all-round knowledge of farming, and was in addition a keen dealer in livestock, might in his lifetime, by adding to his own original patch the patches of those of his neighbours who were improvident or careless, acquire a sizeable farm – say forty, fifty or up to sixty acres.

'Rundale'

If he married, and usually this type of farmer had no difficulty in getting a partner in the days of arranged marriages – and was blessed with a family, the usual procedure was for the daughters to receive a marriage 'portion', and if the sons kept in dad's good graces he willed the farm in fairly equal shares to them.

There you have the cycle beginning over again! The sons had to start off from scratch, trying to acquire acres to make a patch into a farm. Some fell by the wayside, some forsook farming for one of its dependant trades, such as blacksmithing (old-time blacksmiths were often 'horse-doctors' or even 'cow-doctors' as well) or carpentry, and many went to America.

Unmarried or unmarriageable daughters entered domestic service, if possible in Scotland, some few 'hired' as farm servants, and others sought fortune in the United States or Canada.

Eventually, as the standards of living improved, and the money began to flow in from America, Scotland or from the lads who had taken up seafaring, farmers were able to put by a trifle in the bank, and the spread of education made manifest the latent ability of some of their younger sons. The 'trifle' came out of the bank, the clever sons became doctors, barristers or clergymen, and many achieved lasting fame in these professions.

The General Store

Due, in large measure to our lessening dependance upon home-produced goods, together with the increase in the use of imported animal feeding stuffs, small shops or stores, as may of them were rightly named – sprang up all over the countryside and from a few of these evolved the 'Gombeen' type of farmer-shopkeeper-cum-moneylender who proved a worse curse than any tyrannical old-time landlord, especially in the South and West of Ireland. (One or two of Patrick MacGill's stories depict this with stark realism.)

On the whole, the country shopkeeper played a very important part in Glens life, and many a farmer who had a bad season had reason to thank the local store for tiding him over and supplying him with seeds for the next year's effort to recoup his losses.

'Going to Law'

One of the greatest faults of the Glensman of the last and the preceding generation was his litigiousness. He went to law over a 'footery wee bit of a right-of-way', as it was once described in court, and farmers have been known to 'law themselves out' of a couple of snug farms over a matter of access to a field which could have been settled in an hour's sensible discussion.

This right-of-way business is a real bar to neighbourliness. Imagine your neighbour having to take his sheep up to their mountain grazing along a track which is definitely dangerous both for him and the animals, while a couple of hundred yards away is a safe, easy path. You certainly wouldn't wish to see 'Jamie', or 'Hughie', or 'Rabbie' as the case may be – a lad who was your chum at school, perhaps, lying a broken corpse at the foot of the rocks, yet you let him take that risk every time he drives his sheep up or down. Why? Because to allow him to use the safe road might establish his right to walk his sheep where your Da got the court to stop them twenty years ago!

Looked at in this way, it does seem silly, doesn't it?

On the other side of the picture, Jamie has a wee burn running through his land, and of no earthly use to him. It could make all the difference in the world to your upper meadow, but in return for your firmness about the sheep pad (your 'stickinness' he calls it!) he won't allow you to divert it, so in dry weather you have to cart barrels of water when you could be doing something more profitable.

Who benefits?

One explanation given for their tendency to litigation over little is that farmers a generation ago had only lately come into possession of their lands, and in the first pride of ownership were suspicious of anything which might by any stretch of the imagination be conceived as an infringement upon their newly-acquired rights.

Quite a natural feeling, no doubt, after all the years of struggle from serfdom to land ownership, but now that the modern farmer has had time to realise his security of tenure his views regarding a small concession to a neighbour should have broadened.

The Young Farmers' Clubs movement is doing quite a lot to foster the team spirit that lapsed when the 'morrowing' system declined. Morrowing was when a number of farmers combined to help each other in turn with operations such as lint (flax) pulling, bean-shearing, potato digging and the like, its original purpose being to ensure that a landlord did not get a chance to evict a tenant for non-payment of rent. By 'morrowing', the crop was saved and could be sold to raise the necessary money, whereas individual effort would not have sufficed to take full advantage of suitable weather.

To finish our chat about Glens farmers and living. In the old days they even had an old superstitious practice which was believed to win more cases than were won by lawyers!

Somewhere in County Derry there is a place called Banagher (not to be confused with the place in Eire of that name) and if a litigant got hold of some of the sand from here, and managed to sprinkle a little on his opponent's coat while they were in court, the case was as good as won.

What happened if both parties had the brainwave I could not learn.

Itinerant Trades

Shoemaking was an art originally practised in the Glens by itinerants, who visited their clients or prospective clients at certain intervals when they were housed and fed while working at the making or repairing of the footwear of the whole family and sometimes of several neighbouring families as well. The tailor, too, worked on this system, and as regards dressmakers for the ladies – well, most women could use the needle; fashions did not change frequently and one dress a year was about the limit. For bonnets, a girl got one when she reached courting age, one when she married, one (black) if widowed, and one when she reached the stage of the jet-beaded and pink-flowered 'creations' we see in old pictures of the family album.

Creel-making

We have already seen how creels were utilised in the thickening of blankets, but, of course, their real function was that of transporting turf, wrack or potatoes.

The creels of those days were mostly made of plaited hazel rods, some of which were put into the pigs' meat while it was boiling, this treatment making the rods more pliable – though I could never learn whether it had this effect on the porkers!

These rod creels were very strong and could hold a large quantity of turf when it was being transported from the mountain tops down the rough, boulder-strewn paths. Very few, if any, baskets in use were imported and even today you may see growing close to our farmhouses the sally willows from which these baskets were made. Though nowadays they are allowed to straggle or grow all to butt, in the basket-making period they were kept cut back so that they sent forth a profusion of young pliable shoots.

The local name for a whole-time basket-maker was a 'wicker' and the last of these 'McCurry the Wicker' of Ballyeamon, died some years ago.

Some of the work turned out by these basket makers lasted for years, despite the fact that creels were in constant use, winter and summer, and were seldom housed. The baskets were not the only product of their art, as McCurry could make a cupboard, a chair-seat or even a complete and comfortable armchair; also lovely little work-boxes of which some examples may still be found in Ballyeamon Glen.

The potato-baskets, panniers for the backs of donkeys, used in transporting turf or seaweed, and smaller creels for the carriage of turf from stack to fireside, were all home-made.

Cushendall Toy Making

During the twelve years existence of the Cushendall toy industry, orders were also taken for basket-making, an ancillary cottage craft.

Some of the work turned out by the Cushendall toymakers was of so high a quality that orders were received from places as far away as Auckland, New Zealand, and Philadelphia, while in several museums examples of the beautiful craftsmanship of Glens cottagers are preserved.

Credit for the founding of this promising industry must go to the late Miss Barbara McDonnell, who brought to Cushendall a lady who had studied the art and proved herself well fitted to impart it to others. So successful was her teaching that she later admitted the skill of some of her pupils far surpassed her own!

These toys were mostly of wood, many being of the mechanical or working type, such as a Galloping Horse, an ostrich which buried its head, an amusing nursery tale told in wood, The Owl and the Pussy Cat, and a wonderful Magic Mousetrap.

Beautifully dainty and perfectly-proportioned models of Irish jaunting cars and slide-cars were eagerly bought up by American visitors and when Dublin wanted an exact miniature copy of a suite of Chippendale furniture, Cushendall toymakers were given the task which they executed so well that their dolls-house furniture was still on show in Dublin thirty years later.

The outbreak of war in 1914 finished Cushendall toy-making, though orders kept pouring in for its products and the general opinion was that the skill in this art shown by glensfolk should have been utilised during the depression years that preceded the 1939–45 conflict.

Kelp and Iodine

Kelp-gathering – nearly all done during the winter and early spring – was a job that few except longshore dwellers would have cared to tackle. Imagine going out on a cold winter morning and hauling graipfuls and armfuls of tangleweed from the shore up to the sea battery, where it had to lie from some days until it dried and shrank sufficiently to enable it to be put in small cocks on the roadside ditch or stone wall.

These cocks were allowed to lie there for some days until the time when burning was due to commence, then they were carted to a central heap near the kiln. This kiln was a sort of trench fire, made by cutting a hole twelve feet by two feet by three feet deep and then lining it with large stones whose flat sides formed the walls of the trench.

Into this a pile of thin sticks and brushwood was packed,

lighted and when it was well ablaze, the dried seaweed was fed to it, a little at a time, until the whole trench became a glowing mass (older readers may remember the clouds of acrid smoke that used to blow across the Coast Road at this time, being perceptible even miles inland).

More and more weed was added then a couple of large poles, broad at the poking end, were shoved into the melted kelp which was stirred until it glowed like molten iron.

The mass was allowed to cool, which usually took a couple of days, then it was broken out and packed in bags for conveyance to the nearest buying agent, who sent it to the manufacturers of iodine. There were other by-products but when the kelp-gatherers received their payment they weren't interested in the later fate of the stuff.

Iodine, which is one of the most valuable elements in the universe, has not even yet had all its possible uses exhausted. It is one thing without which the human body cannot reach full physical development, and any deficiency in its supply results also in stunted mental growth. The disease known as simple goitre is attributed to iodine deficiency in the food and can be prevented by adding iodised salt to the diet.

One rich source of iodine – from a dietary point of view – is dulse, the tasty seaweed that grows so profusely on the Nine Glens coast of Antrim. When dulse is pulled from the black rocks upon which it grows, dried in the sun on what are called 'spread-grounds', and eaten while still fresh and crackling, its health-giving power is amazing, especially in the case of nervous ailments. The district around Garron Head has acquired a reputation for the best dulse – 'dullace' Belfast people call it – to be got anywhere, and for the past forty years orders have come from England and Scotland for parcels of a couple of pounds or so at time.

Iodine has the power to stop x-rays, and is largely used in radiography. When a photograph of organs or tissues of the body is wanted, iodised oil or other iodised compound is introduced into the body, the tissues thus treated becoming opaque to the x-rays, and showing up in the photograph.

These are only a very few of the uses to which iodine can be put. For instance, the chemist uses iodine largely in the preparation of dyes, and in the world of industrial chemistry the number of products in whose manufacture it figures is constantly increasing.

In any revival of kelp-gathering, modern methods will have to be used. There is no reason why a system for dragging large sleighs loaded with the weed up a reasonably level beach could not be evolved, especially now that so many tractors are available. A company prepared to pay the workers a reasonable wage, and equipped with portable drags for gathering the stuff, could collect as much weed in a few weeks as was formerly got in a whole winter. The drying, too, could be done by erecting stands at places where the wind could get full play at the tangle-weed, thus reducing its weight and bulk and rendering it fit for burning much earlier.

Regarding its use for synthetic fabrics, there are several kinds of seaweed more suitable than others. Instruction in their identification should be given by qualified men, and this almost unlimited source of new material be made available.

The utilising of huge sodium nitrate deposits in Chile put an end to the use of kelp for iodine-making, but the recent discovery that seaweed can be converted into silk stockings and other wear by the art of the chemist promises a new period of prosperity for shore-dwellers.

Black Diamonds at Waterfoot

Reference has already been made to our rich deposits of ore and limestone, but it is not generally known that within a stone's throw of Waterfoot is the spot where a rich seam of the best quality coal was discovered over 90 years ago by the engineers who were boring iron ore there. As soon as this news was conveyed to the firm employing the engineers, orders to close up the shaft were sent post-haste to Waterfoot.

This was done, and the valuable fuel has lain undisturbed since, though pieces are occasionally found washed into the river after floods. Why is this coal not worked? Perhaps the reason is a 'vested interest'!

In what other part of the world would ore, coal, limestone and proximity to sea-transport – all the essentials (except money) for the establishment of a prosperity-bringing industry – be allowed to lie idle?

We are trying to induce cross-Channel industrialists to locate factories here, yet nobody seems interested in all this potential wealth ready to hand.

Our Antrim Dialect

Before continuing our journey we may as well devote a paragraph or two to the dialect of the Nine Glens, a dialect which isn't exactly the same in any two of them, though there are many words and phrases which they have in common. Some years ago Rev. W.F. Marshall, Ulster's greatest authority on dialect, in a series of radio broadcasts under the title 'Ulster Speaks', included illustrations of dialect words in common use in the Glens, using them to show that the Nine Glens speech shows the brands of the Rose, Thistle and Shamrock.

We can easily trace how this came about. The brand of the shamrock was the retention by the native Irish of words from the old tongue when English became the general speech; the brand of the thistle came when the Scottish of the people who settled in the Braid and other surrounding districts became grafted on the still-new language; and the brand of the rose – oldest brand of all – which was the Elizabethan English used by the people such as the Earls of Antrim, who had intercourse with the Royal Court, and whose servants, recruited mostly from the local people, took pattern from their masters' speech.

Another influence, though to a lesser extent, was that of the French settlers who in Huguenot days fled to Ulster and, as mentioned in a previous chapter, were the founders of the linen industry, and this impact of a French-speaking people, coming on top of the influence of the McDonnell clansmen, many of whom were tri-lingual (Gaelic, Scots-English and French), account for the number of words whose French ancestry is obvious.

It sounds like a hotch-potch, but we must bear in mind the fact that English has survived and spread throughout the world, because it has always been most accommodating and receptive to suitable words from other languages, and our distinctive branch of the English tongue is more easily intelligible than, for instance, the dialect of Cumberland or 'Zummerzet'.

One defect we have, our poor delivery, as the visitor is always struck by the fact that we talk in a monotone, what could be a most musical speech being thus reduced to something resembling unintelligent reading. For this defect many people blame the present system in rural schools, where elocution seldom, if ever, figures in the curriculum.

Our dialect can be a little puzzling to a stranger at first, as for instance, when he hears somebody say, 'He's a right omadaun, that!' or 'Jamie's a right sort of boy,' or maybe the reply, 'Och, he's only a gulpin!' Now, an 'omadaun' is a foolish person, and so is a 'gulpin', but the difference between the two is that the 'gulpin' is, in addition to being a bit of a fool, also conceited and self-assertive, whereas the 'omadaun' may become a 'right sort of boy' when he gets 'a bit of wit'.

An amusing use of a local dialect word was when Field-Marshal Sir Alan Brooke (later Baron Alanbrooke) and Field-Marshal Sir Harold Alexander were receiving the freedom of Belfast on October 17, 1945. The Ulster Prime Minister, Sir Basil Brooke, at a banquet given in their honour in the Parliament Buildings, Stormont, said that the teamwork which won the war would help them to win the peace. 'And,' he jokingly added, 'if Britain wants any more field-marshals they can have a 'wheen' of them from us.'

One important item of conversation in these islands is the weather. In the Glens a miserable, wet day is a 'drauchy' day, or in frosty weather it 'has a gey sharp air in it' or is 'snell' or 'there's no hate [heat] in it'. In summer it is 'wild close' or 'gey warm' or 'cowl for this day o' the year'.

A peal of thunder is a 'brattle', a very strong wind is 'a livin' gale' or 'gey wuny'. When the wind is in gusts it is 'gurly'. Snow is 'snaw'; half-melted snow or slush is 'snaw bree'. In wet weather, 'there's nae drouth'.

Smoke is 'reek'; where a house has a thatched roof, the part at the wall is the 'easin''; the latch of the door is the 'snick' or 'sneck'; above the fire is the 'fireboard'; a small stool used by children is a 'creepie'; a stone seat on each side of the fireplace in older type houses was the 'hab' – 'There he sut in the bar spaags (feet), wan fut on ivery hab, maizlin he's shins, an' the oul' woman couldn't get near-han' the fire to harn the preta-oaten she was bakin'.'

Potatoes are 'pretas'; meal is 'male'; porridge 'stirabout'; a quarter section of a round of cake of griddle bread is a 'farl'; a basket is a 'bastick', elastic is 'elasket'; to cook anything in a hurry so that it is only scorched is to 'gie it a scam'.

Eventide is 'duskus', or 'daily-gon', or 'fore-supper' and dawn is 'grey-clear' or 'the first scad o'dawn' or 'skreigh-o-day'.

A collie is a 'coalie'. 'Jamie pulled the bush out o' the slap, him an' the coalie went intill the fiel', an' in a wee while ivery yowe (ewe) was out ower the ditch barrin' wan that fell in the sheugh.'

Where there are many people of the same surname and Christian name in a district, which is a legacy from the clan times, they were identified by special labels, such as 'Red Jamie', 'White Jamie', 'Long Willie', 'Souple Barney', 'Jimmie' or 'Jamie Ban' (white, note the Gaelic term). 'Dan Roe' (ruadh – red) or some territorial designation such as 'Dan o' the Hill', 'Wullie o' the Black Burn', and even 'Wullie's Dan's Jamie' is likely to occur, though the most complicated name I have heard went something like this: 'Wullie Tam o' the Midgey Corner's son's woman's brother's wean.'

Sort that out!

In ordinary conversation a Glensman will refer to his wife as 'my woman' and his children are the 'weans' though matriarchy is not unknown.

To the 'weans' their father is 'our oul' fella' and their mother is 'the oul' lady' – but do not imagine that any want of respect for their parents is to be inferred from this! Nowhere do mother and father get more real love and obedience from their children than in the homes of the Glens, and to few places did the 'Americay money' flow back in greater profusion during the days of unrestricted emigration. Even today in Green Point, Brooklyn, the accents of the Glens can be clearly distinguished, and in parts of California Glens folk have formed little colonies of their own, while Montreal, Quebec and Ottawa have all large numbers of Antrim Coast emigrants or their descendants.

Have you ever heard of the 'beverage' of a hat (pronounced 'beeverage')? This is what happens when a Glens girl enters a room wearing a new hat for the first time: the young man who spots her is entitled to 'gie her the beverage o' it', i.e. kiss her, and the chance is seldom let slip! Sometimes two of them may each imagine he saw it first but a diplomatic young lady can easily settle that argument and please both of them!

Dr William Grant, editor of the *Scottish National Dictionary*, wrote to a Belfast newspaper in which an article of mine appeared, pointing out that the word 'beverage' was in use in some parts of Scotland, with meaning something the same as ours, yet the expression (and custom) are as unknown in any other part of Ulster as growing mistletoe!

I once heard a middle-aged farmer describing one of his infrequent visits to a cinema. 'Thon puke!' said he, 'with the mouth like a Christie minstrel, an' the swinged (singed) eyebrows, she give me a scunner, she did!'

To 'take a scunner' at anything means to develop a deep repugnance to it, a dislike that would almost make you 'boke' (retch).

'It was that dark I couldn't see a stime' (ray of light) is another common saying, and it is quite on the cards that on a night like that the traveller suddenly heard a 'wild skreighing' coming from the side of the road, followed by a 'fisslin' (rustling) in the hedge, then out of the darkness, enveloped in a glow of light, came a banshee and perched on her 'hunkers' (haunches) on a nearby wall!

If you are ever in the Nine Glens at mushroom time, you may be warned not to pull 'puddockstools', which warning may not be needed as you knew toadstools long ago, but you may be excused for not knowing the difference between a 'puddockstool' and a 'puddocksteel' (mushroom).

The person who digs up a large potato in his garden and may be 'tovey' (i.e. inclined to boast) about it is likely to be reminded that over-large spuds are mostly 'bose' (hollow).

'A 'brave' sort of a boy,' a 'brave' wean, a 'brave' hizzy have nothing to do with the courage of the young man, child or girl thus referred to. Brave, one of the words of French derivation, in our country means a fine young man or a good sort of girl or a well-developed child. There is, of course, a 'brave' day which is not altogether a good day but fair to middling.

Perhaps Mary Ellen and her chum Maggie Kate are out for a walk and meet two boys. If Mary Ellen – either innocently or of malice aforethought – shoves her arm through that of Davie and walks him off leaving her with Willie (for whom she has 'no gra') it is possible that the upshot may be – as described by Willie:

Maggie Kate 'strunted' an' hardly opened her mouth, till at last I could thole it no longer.

'Maggie Kate,' sez I, 'are you like that doll m'sister's wean hez?'

'What d'ye mane,' sez she.

'I mane this,' sez I, puttin' my arm roun' her. 'D'ye only talk when ye're squeezed?'

She landed me a 'sotherer' of a 'dunner' on the 'lug' made it 'bizz' for half an hour after but she laughed all the same, an' I'm to see her the morra night.'

In wet weather, when the wells become muddy looking with the floods, if you bring in a can or a bucket of water you will be advised to let it 'shire' before using it, that is, to leave it aside until the solid matter or sediment sinks to the bottom. A 'go' of water means one visit to the well whether you carry one or two receptacles. 'I brought two 'goes' of water' is a common phrase.

'As light in the loof as a weaver's (pronounced 'waver's') kiss' is a very apt description of a gentle-handed nurse, 'loof being the palm of the hand, and 'weaver's kiss' being the almost imperceptible touch of a spider when hanging from its thread.

A 'scradyin' is a small, undersized person, a 'grogach' is a leprechaun or Puck-ish type of fairy, reputed to spend most of his time sitting over a crock of gold and mending small shoes (or brogues) as a blind. A 'brose' is a big, fat person, an uncomplimentary reference except when applied to a baby. On the other hand, it's a 'carried-away lookin' crathur' is used to refer to a baby that looks unlovely and underfed like one that the fairies had left – a changeling, in fact.

Until recently newts were dreaded by us as they were believed to enter the inside of anyone who drank from the pond or well they frequented.

'Mankeepers', we call them, and the story goes that a man who had drunk from a mankeeper-infested pool felt strange movements in his tummy shortly afterwards.

Becoming alarmed, he consulted a local wise woman who advised him to fast for twenty-four hours then to eat three salt herrings and go and lie beside the pool with his mouth over it. He did exactly as he was told with the result that no less than seven very thirsty newts hopped out of his inhospitable inside and dived gladly into their native element!

'Sonsy' is a woman who is built on generous lines, or 'curves'. 'Crabb-ed' is cross and 'carnaptious' conveys almost the same meaning. 'Cassey' is the (usually) paved yard in front of a farmhouse. 'In spales' – in fragments.

A group of houses up to about half-a-dozen is called a 'clachan' – a name commonly used in the Scottish Highlands – but in the northern Glens such as Glenaan or Glendun the name for any small collection of dwellings is 'a town of houses'. Here, too, we have 'ing' pronounced 'een' as walkeen, talkeen, courteen, etc., and another notable point about Glenaan or Glendun English is its resemblance to the English of the Hebrides. This, of course, is due to the fact that until less than a century ago the language of both the Hebrides and the Northern Glens was mainly Gaelic and both people speak English with a copy-book correctness that sounds pedantic to others who have a more slipshod enunciation.

About Glenarm and Carnlough the Lowland Scottish infiltration is obvious. A native of either village says 'cannae' or 'dinnae' for cannot or don't, uses 'no' for not – A'm no gonna gie him ony mair' (I'm not going to give him any more). The funny part about it is that Glenarm is divided into two classes of speakers, the users of Elizabethan and fairly grammatical modern English and the lowland 'Burns' dialect users.

It is interesting, at a fair, regatta or other congregation of

Nine Glens folk to hear the diversity of dialects and to attempt to place the speakers. It can be done to within a mile or two!

Talking of fairs reminds me that these once-important events have ceased to play as great a part in Glens life as they did, due to the Government control of prices and also to the fact that dealers do not now wait until the animals are brought to fair or market, but with improved transport facilities can buy on the farm and have the animals or produce delivered to suit themselves. Our fairs are but shadows of the olden events, when they were to occasion not only of buying and selling, but also of merry-making afterwards.

An old-time fair was very enjoyable if a bit noisy. The animals were scattered in groups over the 'Fair Hill' while buyers and sellers engaged in animated discussion. The ballad singers, with a crowd around them, 'rendered' the latest songs, many of their own composition, dealing with the doings of 'Tommy the Toff-t' or 'Willie Wilson's Wake', or a regatta or horse-race, the various – whack-fol-de-dols' being chorused by the listeners.

Then there was the congregation of young folk of both sexes for the twice-yearly 'hiring fair' when they either changed their master or mistress for the ensuing six months or agreed to stay on for another term. This was their one day of liberty, when the girls donned the finery that had lain in camphor-scented boxes, not even being produced for the couple of hours granted them to attend their church on Sundays. The boys, very self-conscious in their 'fine' boots (yellow for preference) and their blue suits with unaccustomed collars feeling as if they might choke them, meandered – or 'dandered' as they themselves called it – about, casting sheeps-eyes at pretty damsels who, missing none of these glances, but apparently intent only upon the chatter they were having with other girls, could yet send a devastating glint from a bonny eye that reduced some lad to a humble hanger-on at that night's dance.

Only one of these big fairs remains, and even that is shorn of much of its former importance, though the song, *The Ould Lammas Fair of Ballycastle* has helped to bring more sightseeing visitors to that attractive little town on the last Tuesday of August each year. (*The Ould Lammas Fair* was sung at a Royal Command performance in 1937.)

5

Rough Riding on the Road to Ballycastle

It was a fresh, cold, but pleasant November day as I left Cushendun and started my 'hike' to Torr, six miles or so away. The first mile took me past what was the home of the late Lord Cushendun, 'Glenmona', on our left and away on the right was the curve of Cushendun bay, Rockport (Moira O'Neill's old home and later the residence of the late J. Humbert Craig, the celebrated artist) showing white against the dark background of the hill.

Cushendun has been the birthplace of many famous people, Moira O'Neill being one of these, but in more modern days we had the McSparran family, one of whom, James, was a celebrated KC and MP for Mourne in the Northern Ireland Parliament.

Another brother, Rev. J. McSparran, was the founder of the St John Bosco Boys' Club, a club whose young members have gained many laurels in the amateur boxing ring and can claim to be one of the pioneers of the Boys' Club movement in Belfast.

Another celebrated figure was Dan McAuley – better known by 'Dan Mick' – who into a comparatively short lifetime packed more adventures than usually fall the lot of a couple of adventure-seekers.

Educated at a Belfast college, and destined for a church career, he felt the call of the sea so strongly that he ran away and joined a schooner in which he served several years. He later sat for and obtained his master's 'ticket', and sailed as mate both in sail and steam. He then spent some years in the United States, came home, and with his wife started a restaurant on Glasgow's Broomielaw where he did a most thriving business. After the 1914–18 war he bought a farm at Nappan, Garronpoint, and tried to settle down, but the death of his wife, a young woman, unsettled him again and he sold the farm, bought a travelling cinema outfit and for years travelled all over Ireland. The rapid growth of new cinema halls drove him off the road and he returned to Cushendall where at the time of his death he had a flourishing coal trade.

Shane O'Neill's Cairn

The climb out of Cushendun was steep and despite the coolness of the fresh breeze from the sea I was soon warm and wasn't sorry when I spotted on the left the large cairn that is supposed to mark the place where Shane O'Neill met his end. I negotiated some barbed wire and saw the red sandstone blocks set at intervals around the cairn.

The first, facing towards the road, was inscribed 'Sean O'Neill, 1567', then, taking them according to dates, 'Francis Joseph Bigger, 1908', Eoin MacNeill, 1908', 'Liam Bulfin, 1909', 'Shane Leslie, 1910', 'Sean Gall, 1911' and 'Liam MacGiollabrid, 1912'.

The view from here was superb and no chieftain could have chosen a more fitting place to end a turbulent career (not that Shane O'Neill appears to have had much choice in the matter!).

I was now near the top of the long drag and before me I could see the road winding very steeply downwards, and soon I was passing the Crook, as it is called, near Corrymeela, a spot which must at a time have been much more populous than at present as there were numerous remains of stone houses all around, buildings whose roofless 'wall-steads' spoke of homes now abandoned to wind, weather and rats. Whether these were the habitations of victims of the 1845–7 Famine, whether the drift to the towns had carried off the young folk, or – what seems more likely – they had left the poor soil to seek a better livelihood in the fertile lands of the United States or Canada, I know not, but such ruins are seldom seen in any prosperous countryside.

A Helping Hand

While toiling up the next hill, the surface of rough 'screenings' on the road making walking an uncomfortable experience, I heard behind me an unexpected sound, the roar of a motor-bicycle. The rider passed me, then signalled that he was going to stop and when I came up to him he asked me how far I was going. 'Torr,' said I.

'Would you like a lift? I'm going to near Torr,' he said, adding, 'the pillion seat isn't very soft, especially for this road, but it's better than walking.'

Did I accept his kindly offer? I did, with alacrity, and soon we were travelling along at a speed which might on a normal road have appeared slow but on this pot-holed and stone-strewn high-way seemed positively reckless, especially on 'Dan Nancy's Brae'!

The seat was a little hard especially over the potholes, but Mr Pat Hamilton of Tornamona knew how to handle a motorbike and, despite his concentration upon this task, could find time to direct my attention to the places of interest en route.

There was a slang expression current for some time, 'that shook you!' or as we put it in the Glens, 'that shuk ye!' Well, that ride certainly 'shuk' me; nevertheless it was with regret that I parted from Pat at his journey's end, a mile or so from Torr.

The pleasant slopes around Cushendun must at one time have been well wooded as names like Beaghs (birches) and Unshinagh (Ashgrove) and Tornamoney indicate the presence of timber, but apart from their actual meaning these names have a certain musical sound all their own. We have names like Claudy, Drumfaskey, Drumnasmere, Knocknacollesky, Legadaughten or Dunourgan that excite curiosity as to their meaning and usually the translation is not disappointing.

Mention of Dunourgan is a reminder that Dunourgan figured in one of the most amusing Nine Glens ballads ever written, Dan McGonnell's *The Courtin' of Henry Pat*.

This tells the adventures of a bachelor, one Henry Pat, who is long past his best, though, maybe not at his worst, and who is suddenly seized with an amorous notion and sets out in search of a wife. Dressed in the 'height of style', as he fondly imagines, he makes a few advances which are repulsed – but we'll let Dan tell the story himself:

The Courtin' of Henry Pat

> You marrying young maids and youthful brides
> Who dwell by hill and glen,
> And females all around Cushendall
> A-looking out for men;
> Keep up your hearts and take advice,
> Give up the country 'brat',
> And look for the monied farmer men
> Like sporting Henry Pat.

This sparkling youth, a farmer boy
Of sixty-nine or so
Had lost his dearest loved one
In the days of long ago;
He sold his farm and stock and crop
Then bought a sealskin hat –
Where was the roving bachelor
As proud as Henry Pat?

Susanna spoke to Henry, and said:
'Now, brother dear,
Good counsel I will give to you,
You know it is sincere:
Look out for youth and beauty,
With gold and this and that,
And the lord may send you, by and by,
A little Henry Pat.

'Thank you, kindly sister,
I've already tried the game,
But youth and beauty will not have
My polished-up old frame;
When I salute a courting maid
By taking off my hat,
The hairless crown betrays the age
Of brother Henry Pat.'

He looked at grand Glenariff
And said, 'I'll not try you.'
Then hopped across the brown Glendun

To get a better view;
He down right through Dunourgan came,
And the maidens wondered what
Was he the boy they'd heard about,
The famous Henry Pat.

He bought a fine umbrella,
The cost was four-and-six,
Then up he went to Mallinskea
To sport about at Dick's;
Folk thought he was a circus clown,
'Where did you get that hat?'
But Mary Murphy knew the boy,
Her lover, Henry Pat.

This handsome maid, Miss Murphy,
Was prudent, wise and shy,
But Henry's gold was glittering
In greedy Mary's eye.
Friends asked her would she take him,
She answered, 'Will I what?
Wed the Lord of Antrim's Glens,
My lover, Henry Pat?'

A couple of verses follow, describing H.P.'s doings in his efforts
to impress the girls, then –

But Henry's sporting, spending days
Were sudden bound to end.
A gipsy warned him oftimes

His mate the Lord would send.
He dreaded some ill-looking one,
Not the handsome Eamon cat [Ballyeamon]
Who stretched her paw and caught her prey,
First prize – Old Henry Pat.

Old bachelors get here a bit of advice 'not to let their hearts to down, for they ne'er got 'chucked' who had the pluck of sporting Henry Pat.' We learn that 'Proud Henry has got wedded, and his sporting days are past', then comes the following –

I hope the first will be a boy,
If the Lord does so allow;
I'll willing act as sponsor then
And take a solemn vow
To train him well in poetry,
I know he'll be no 'flat',
With his mother Mary Murphy
And his father Henry Pat.

Queer Diving Adventures

It was near Dunourgan, on a wild winter's night, about ninety years ago, with a snowstorm raging that the *Taymouth Castle* was wrecked, all hands being lost.

The bodies that came ashore were interred in one grave at Layde, where the large mound is still visible.

The salvaging of what remained of value on the *Taymouth Castle* was the first important job undertaken by the Murray brothers of Waterfoot, the salvage and diving experts who afterwards made a name for themselves by the recovery of articles of value from *Clementine* (Belgian Royal Yacht sunk in Red Bay during the 1914–18 war). Another of their salvage feats was on the *Lake Champlain*, driven ashore at Cushendun in June 1886, and their list of successes included the *Ancoria, Cometa, Islington Firth* and I*rishman*. They also did much good work at the sinking of foundations of piers from Tramore (Waterford) to Glenarm.

About 1917 one of the Murrays had an experience which would have tried the nerve of most people.

While at work on a wreck he had occasion to force open the door of a cabin and when he entered it he was engaged in an examination of it when a pair of boots above his head came into his range of vision. He turned his light upwards and there was a corpse encased in two life-jackets stuck like a huge fly to the ceiling!

The life-jackets by their buoyancy were keeping it suspended in the water which filled the cabin!

It was while working at the sunken *Clementine* that Alex Murray had an adventure which resulted in his never again donning a diving suit.

In his own words, he had just descended and was making his way over the hull when a monstrous something attacked him.

A terrific fight for life ensued, and but for the fact that those in the boat above realised that he was in some difficulty and acted promptly, he would almost certainly have fallen victim to what he described as a twenty-foot-long creature, eel-like, and with a mane round its neck like that of a horse!

He was unconscious when hauled up and the memory of his horrifying experience remained fresh until his death some years ago.

Culraney

From Cushendun to Torr would be too much of a jump without mention of the very interesting stretch of country in between, so we'll retrace our steps a little.

Due to the fact that the only good road from Cushendun to Ballycastle is the one that passes over Carey mountain past Loughareema, very few writers seem to have got to know anything about the road ('loaning' describes it better) that follows the coastline to Torr.

Rev. J. Smith, the well-known antiquary and folklorist, who was CC for some time at Glenravel, is a notable exception. He has published much interesting data about this corner of the Glens, some of which has appeared in the *Down and Connor Historical Society's Journal*.

In a chat I had with Mr James McDonnell ('The Mason' as he was called locally), he told me some little-known things about the people who lived there in the first half of the last century, including exciting tales of the adventures of the old-time schoonermen who sailed from Cushendun Bay.

These men all had small farms, and it was the custom for groups of neighbours to combine and acquire a schooner. Having put in their crops, they then manned the little vessel and sailed away for 'furrin parts'. It was usual for them to carry a pilot as far as Land's End (Cornwall), where he was put ashore.

After that their relatives heard of them no more until they sailed again into Cushendun Bay in the autumn, their holds full of cargo (or maybe their pockets full of money instead!).

Sometimes their arrival was timed for the hours of darkness, when they slipped furtively to the vicinity of some little creed, lowered their dinghy and rowed ashore, loaded to gunwale with wine, brandy or tobacco – or maybe all three!

The tale is told of one such schooner making shorewards when she was intercepted by a vigilant revenue man, whose cutter ran almost alongside and hailed her.

An answering 'Ahoy!' came from the vessel.

'Where are you going?' queried the coastguard officer, an Englishman.

'Fish man me. No Ingli!' came the reply.

'Blast it!' muttered the officer, 'the fellows can't speak anything but Irish – what cargo have you?'

A – to him – unintelligible stream of Gaelic was the answer but he noticed one of his men laughing heartily.

'What is the joke?' he demanded, 'do you understand him?'

'She says she hass no cargo only brandy, sugar and tobacco,' answered the man addressed (a Highlander), 'that iss the shoke.'

'A mad Glens fisherman!' said the officer, 'let him go. If he had any contraband aboard he wouldn't be so ready to admit it.'

Let him go they did and it was some time later when it was all safely disposed of that the Englishman learned to his chagrin that the 'mad' Glensman had landed a full cargo of contraband right under his nose!

A few even more adventurous spirits were not content to confine themselves to a voyage lasting from seed-time to harvest, but bravely set their course for the New World, whence those who survived the many hazards of such a tour brought back cargoes that fetched good prices in the markets of London and Liverpool. It sounds incredible, yet there are well-authenticated accounts of some of these Glens schooners having made the passage round the Horn, then up the Pacific Coast to Chile and Peru, returning safely with valuable cargoes and many souvenirs of their exploration!

Culraney Chapel was started about 1850 by Fr Patrick Starkey, and finished by Fr John Garland, being dedicated to Dr Denvir on September 16, 1855.

The majority of modern churches are set in what is known as a commanding position, but in the case of Culraney the site chosen appears to have been the most sequestered available. Below it the rocks undulate to the edge of a cliff fronting the sea, and behind it steep slopes stretch up to the heather. The outstanding features are rocks, bare or thinly clad with heather, a clump of whins or gorse showing when in bloom as the only patch of bright colour.

There is, however, a superb view across the Channel, and on a clear day Scotland seems a very near neighbour (it is actually about 15 or 16 miles as the plane flies).

James Studdert Moore, already mentioned during our talk on Nine Glens bards, wrote a poem that well expresses the thoughts of one of the old-time fishermen or schoonermen as he sailed away on one of his hazardous voyages. Here it is:

Slainte! Cushleake

> Slainte! Cushleake, methinks I hear
> The fisherman's anthem once again
> Ring round the headlands, wild and clear,
> The cheery ring of the old refrain
> Oft as it echoed round by Torr,
> Oft as it ran o'er cliff and hollow,
> Oft as it sounded round that shore
> Slainte! Cushleake, O baile go baile!

Oh! for the warm, sweet summer night
When leaves are green on the woods of Clona;
Oh! for the wild waves leaping white
On the long dark point of Tornamona;
Oh! for a good seaworthy craft,
With sails well set, and the wind to follow;
The foaming breakers well abaft
Then Slainte! Cushleake, O baile go baile!

Though I may ne'er again behold
The sunset glow on old Kintyre
Tinging the rugged cliffs with gold
Till all the headlands seem afire,
Though I on Ailsa Craig no more
May see it gleam like rosy halo,
Or shine on Sanda's distant shore,
Slainte! Cushleake, O baile go baile!

The Big Shower

Old residents in the neighbourhood still speak with awe of what they call 'The Big Shower', which occurred over fifty years ago. It certainly was a shower, consisting of hailstones bigger than pigeon's eggs which broke windows, killed hens, ducks and geese by the hundred, and in one case smashed the window beside which a baby was sleeping and severely injured the child's face before help could arrive. (That child, James McDonnell informed me, belonged to a family from whom the well known Ballymena merchants in Broughshane Street are descended.)

A description of the scene on the mountainside was given to me by a brother of James McDonnell. 'I was out that day on the mounteen,' he said, 'a bit of a lad in the bare feet. It was a grand warm day in the month of June. All of a sudden it got dark, and the sky turned nearly black, then down came lumps of ice like eggs and drops of water like the dregs you'd throw out of a bucket! It didn't last long, but when I came out from where I was sheltereen in a peat bank, and made for home, it was odd to see all the ground shineen white like snow in the sunshine – but the oddest thing of the lot was to feel my feet sinkeen through the icy stuff on to the warm ground below it!'

Crops were destroyed, people running for shelter arrived with their ears badly cut up and hands covered with black bruises received when trying to save their heads from the aerial bombardment and it was days before the icy coating melted off the ground.

The queerest part about this freak shower was that it fell only within a space of a few miles. It came from a westerly direction ('From Derry way,' one old-timer told me) and was in the shape of a wedge with the broad end in front.

It passed out over the North Channel but there is no mention of it having struck anywhere on the Scottish coast so it seems to have been a treat reserved for the Cushleake and Culraney folk!

Some of the place-names from Cushendun to near Torr are Cross Skreen, Cashel, Ligadaughten, Carnaneigh, The Green Hill and Farranmacallan, in that order.

In a spot where vegetation appears to have a struggle to exist, it is strange to come upon 'The Green Hill', a rounded slope whose surface, even in mid-winter (snow excepted) is a beautiful emerald green. This phenomenon may be accounted for by the presence of some element in the soil that is conducive to the growth of herbage but whatever the reason, The Green Hill is a most pleasant sight.

You remember that before we went into reverse to have a better look at the Culraney district, we had reached a spot not far from Torr Head (thanks to a 'sail' – as Glensfolk call a 'ride' or a 'lift' – on a motorcycle).

Let us get back there and continue our journey.

Torr Head

As I dismounted from Pat Hamilton's pillion seat I felt like a bronco-buster after a rodeo. However, this feeling soon passed when I saw, about a mile away, towards the shore, the dark point of Torr, with the Coastguard Lookout Station crowning its summit.

Turning to the right, at where a signpost said Torr Head $^1/_2$ mile, and passing a snug farmhouse on the way, I went through a gateway and along a steep loaning to where a gaunt ruin stood, the remains of what was once a group of comfortable coastguard homes (they were burnt down during 'The Troubles').

From here a line of white posts was visible, extending zig-zag fashion up to the Station, and where the loaning ended at a small wooded gate, I began the ascent by a path marked with these posts and a wire rope stretched between them. Breathless I reached the tip, and after a few minutes' parley at the door was admitted to the comfortable and spotlessly-clean Station living-room, where preparations for departure seemed to be underway.

My first thought was that the place was closing down, but the coastguards laughed when I mentioned this and informed me that after a week on the Head they are relieved by another watch and spend the next week in Ballycastle.

Although in my seafaring days I had often passed close to Torr when beating up for the entrance to the Sound of Rathlin, yet it was my first time ashore there. It brought back memories when I saw a coaster passing up north, examined her through the powerful binoculars and saw that she was the steamer *Lakewood* (Messrs Dorey, formerly of Guernsey) likely bound for Londonderry. (Later I learned from her skipper, Captain McGahey, that this surmise was correct.)

I saw some of the boxes of war material, such as Air Force flares, all American, which had been washed up about the beach here. Very interesting was the story my hosts told me of the time the Mine Disposal Squad exploded one of the dangerous big balls which had drifted ashore just below the Head.

To get down to it the bomb-busters had to use the chain which fishermen here utilised for generations when descending to fish or returning again from the shore (women, I was told, used it also when carrying up 'skeiltigs' full of wrack . ('Skeiltig' is a large piece of hessian, like a 2 cwt bran bag cut lengthwise, and used in carrying seaweed for kelp or manure.)

Torr Head was called Dunbarach (Barach's Fort) by the people living near there prior to the erection of the Coastguard Station (1818), and some standing stones up at Torr West were 'Barach's Finger-stones' which he was supposed to have thrown at another 'giant' on Balllyucan, though they fell short.

Barach, King Conor's unscrupulous courtier, must have been confused by tradition with some of the mythological giants. Finn MacCumhaill (MacCoole) is an example of real personage whose authentic deeds were magnified by tradition into legendary lore, and the same seems to have happened to Barach.

(When we reach Ballycastle we'll hear more about Barach.)

Cave Exploration

The caves at Staffa, one of which is Fingal's Cave, 227 feet long, are famous, but underneath Torr Head is a cave that has never been fully explored, and may some day become just as well known as the Hebridean ones which it is said to resemble very much in some respects. One of the Torr residents, having informed me that the cave was partially explored in his youthful days by the Very Rev. J. Cannon McLister, PP, VF, of Ballymena, I called with him and found him most genial and helpful in every way. He was disposed to make light of his adventurous trip on which he was accompanied by a lad named Rainey, but one could gather that it was indeed a hazardous undertaking for two youths equipped only with candles.

Canon McLister said that after traversing the outer section one had to creep through a small tunnel-like part to get to another large chamber which contained several pits – presumably the pits in which local tradition says the smugglers of wines, brandy and tobacco cached their stocks until a favourable opportunity came to dispose of them. Getting round these pits (which were likely left open as traps for revenue men or any over-inquisitive visitors), the flickering candlelight only accentuating the darkness beyond its range, must have been a test of nerve. The explorers pushed on, however, until the air got so bad that the lights refused to burn, and they had to retrace their steps.

Some years afterwards, away up on the hillside, a local man was poking his fire one night when fire, fireplace and all disappeared before his eyes! The ground had opened and swallowed it! The Canon's theory is that the house had by chance been erected on the site of an old souterrain, but the local people persisted in believing that the fireplace dropped into the Torr cavern! The entrance to the cave is covered at full tide, but it is easy of access from half ebb until half flow, allowing what should be ample time for exploring it.

Earlier in these notes I mentioned the unusually large number of ruins of former houses and in the course of our chat Canon McLister asked me if I had noticed this. He then went on to explain that most of the residents in this once populous district had migrated to Glasgow, or, as in the case of the McKay family, gone to New Zealand, or, adopting seafaring as a career, had made new homes in seaport towns.

He regretted his inability to remember the many old folk-tales he had heard as he had left the district at an age when such tales made little impression on his mind, but he mentioned one or two old-timers who might be regarded as 'seannachies', and recalled that the district was famed for wells whose water had various properties, one in particular being in great demand for use in buttermaking.

I also gleaned the interesting fact that a local ancient burying-ground, which from its name 'Killowen' must have been at one time the site of a church, was originally much larger than at present, as part of it was incorporated in his farm by a Scot called Rainey, who turned up some human remains when ploughing it.

Lord Cushendun and New Road

Regarding a decent road round Torr, the Canon said that the agitation for its construction had been going on for many years, the late Lord Cushendun (Ronald McNeill) having been one of the numerous influential people whose efforts to that end were unable to get the County Council to move in the matter. This want of a road suitable for transporting their produce was partly

responsible for the exodus of the farming community, another
contributory factor being the poor harbour facilities for
fishermen.

In the old days farmers combined to buy a boat and nets,
manned her themselves and went fishing, sometimes – like the
present-day Breton fishermen – making as far as the cod banks
of Newfoundland, whence they brought back catches of which
they sold the major part, some being retained, cured and used all
winter to 'keep them in kitchen', along with some home-cured
bacon, and the killing of an occasional sheep.

(The travelling shop didn't exist in those days!)

There is another cave in the south side of Torr, entry to
which is obtained by a narrow passage between two large rocks,
one of which projects to seaward of the cave. The visitor is likely
to think that the wall he meets a little way from the entrance has
been put there to bar his further progress, but the truth is that
this barrier was found necessary owing to the number of sheep
that wandered into the dark inner recesses of the cavern and
could not make their way back, being found later dead of
starvation.

Like the Garronpoint 'Cove', this place also has a tradition of
a 'piper' who entered it gaily playing his pipes and was heard a
couple of days later underneath where a man was ploughing,
sadly droning a lament!

Most of such tales have a foundation in fact, and the
recurrence of this story in connection with so many caves may
possibly be attributable to the old storytellers' attempts to place
locally the scene of one of the ancient Irish 'Tales' called *Uatha*,
or *Caves*.

This story, *Uath Belagh Conglais* it is named, tells of a prince of Leinster who lived in the first century AD. A renowned huntsman, he entered, while hunting, the cave which has since been called after him, 'Belach Conglais' (Baltinglass, County Cork), disappeared there and was never seen again.

There are only a few families from the point of Torr right along to the lip of Murlough, though there are numerous indications of former occupation. Again the need for a better road can be seen, as it is obvious that the value of all this district for food production could be greatly increased by better transport facilities.

During the days when there was a less sparse population, the only method of goods transportation possible was to convey half loads to the tops of the hills, leave them off there, return for the other half, load up and start for market, the double journey entailing the loss of half a day, in addition to losing the higher first-of-market prices. On roads with well-engineered gradients, all this could have been avoided.

The second Report of the Commissioners for the Extension and Improvement of Public Works in Ireland, published over a hundred years ago, contained this paragraph: 'Wherever a new road is constructed, flourishing farms at once spring up, and the carts of the countrymen press on the heels of the roadmakers as the work advances. In Ireland, where agriculture affords the principal means of national wealth, the opening of new districts by the construction of roads upon well-considered plans, gives an accumulative source of productive industry an immense power and at little cost.'

Have we not advanced even a little since then?

In 1945 a stretch of road in the Murlough district disappeared into the bowels of the earth! It is surmised that it was constructed over the shell of an old mine shaft which collapsed – though one might be forgiven for surmising that Nature thought such an antiquated thoroughfare had hindered local evolution long enough!

Of all the places that fringe Antrim's bay-indented coast, none is so remote or inaccessible as Murlough. This is partly due to the fact that most of the main roads seem to have been constructed by people who didn't know Murlough existed, and partly due to the bay itself being useless as a haven in the prevailing gales.

The early roadmakers who bypassed Murlough are to be excused as it is situated at the bottom of a very steep hillside but that difficulty can be overcome nowadays when a car can go almost 'anywhere puss can go' if the road itself is good.

Hikers have become quite a feature of our landscape, and a very welcome one too, but there are cases when even the experienced hiker feels that he can echo the words of the late James Gorman in his *Hiker's Lament*.

Hiker's Lament

I'm bound for the city, an object of pity,
The reason I'll try to explain;
I've sores on my back through humpin' a pack
And I'll never go hiking again.

I'm nearly distracted, my stomach's contracted
And wrinkled I'm sure it must be;
I must eat to expand it or else I'll be landed
In Layde with a tombstone o'er me.

I'm all bone and skin, legs scraggy and thin,
And I'm certain my blood is impure;
I must pare my corns and pick out the thorns
And try a 'rheumatics' cure.

I'm now showing bunions the size of small onions
And ingrowing nails that show pain;
I'm losing much weight and lots of 'consate'
And feel far more humble and sane.

For my present condition I blame malnutrition
An ill with all hikers I share;
And that's what I reap, when I live on the cheap,
A few buns and some fresh mountain air.

To vary the fare I eat a large share
Of berries I pick on my way;
Though not satisfying, still there's no denying
They're something for nothing each day.

Sometimes as a treat, feeling weak on my feet,
Extravagance takes a new turn;
I've a pen'orth of cheese which I munch at my ease
And a draught from the nearest wee burn.

Nevermore will I boast of a tramp round the Coast,
Or the ozone mixed up with the air;
Little to eat, no butcher's meat,
And the fun that I failed to find there.

If I ever come back I'll be minus a pack,
And clad as a rational sight;
In my automobile not an ache will I feel,
And I'll choose my hotel every night.

I've bartered my health, added none to my wealth,
And hiking's all right for a cod;
But I've made up my mind, pleasure elsewhere I'll find,
Till I'm planted right under the sod.

Dr James McDonnell, the famous physician who founded the first fever hospital in Great Britain or Ireland (at Belfast) had a farm at Murlough to which he retired when he needed a rest from his manifold duties. Although born in the vicinity of Cushendall and always keeping a warm spot in his heart for his native glen, he yet loved his Murlough home, and many a long walk he used to take around the lovely spot, 'culloguing' with the local people, collecting articles of antiquarian interest and noting the wealth of rare plants and flowers that grew in unfrequented nooks about the hillsides.

If ever the road is improved and access to Murlough's made easier, the place is bound to become popular with lovers of the picturesque and people who like to feel the unrestricted lash of the sea wind whipping the colour to their cheeks.

Studying Rare Birds

The keen ornithologist has here a rich field for exploration, as Murlough (like North Rathlin) is the habitat of birds found nowhere else in Antrim. Seals, too, play around the sea-caves in numbers comparable only to what I have seen at Loop Head, Co. Clare.

Which recalls an amusing incident that occurred near there. A party of visitors, including two ladies, one young and one not so young and both unmarried, were being rowed around the Loop Head shore near some caves. As they approached the entrance to a large cavern the elderly lady, who had been seated facing the shore, suddenly turned round and started to gaze intently seaward.

'Oh! Look! Look!' said the younger lady. 'I refuse to look!' said the other rather tartly, which surprised them all as they were being treated to the spectacle of dozens of seals diving into the water from their various resting-places on the side of the cavern.

Later, when they returned to land, the elder lady confessed to the younger that she had mistaken the figures entering the water for a number of 'unclothed bathers' who had been taken unawares and were seeking the covering of the sea at the boat's approach!

St Moluag's Murlough Home

St Moluag, the great friend of the more-famous St Brendan the navigator (who, it is claimed, was before Columbus in discovering America) had a hermit's retreat at Drumnakeel, Murlough, though he had founded many churches at different spots on the Scottish side and was Abbot of Lismore, Firth of Lorne.

The Mull of Cantyre (or Kintyre, as it is sometimes spelt) appears on a clear day only a very short row away, but the rower who tries it and does not know how the tides run and their strength may find himself at Larne Lough or the Rhynns of Islay Point before he is picked up! Despite these swift currents flowing to and from the North Atlantic, the hardy Scottish and Irish seamen carried on a regular trade, crossing in their small vessels with cattle, pigs, sheep and the strong little Highland ponies from which the 'Cushendall' was later developed.

It was through this trade that the fair at Ballycastle rose to such importance, and its decline to its present proportions started from the introduction of the regular sail (and later steam) shipping services between Londonderry and the Clyde.

Glens-Glasgow Intercourse

There are many descendants of the Antrim Glensfolk about Campbelltown and in parts of Bute, names like O'Hara occurring frequently but today any intercourse is mostly through Glasgow and the people who have settled there from the Glens. During the 'Fair' holidays of Glasgow hundreds of Glens-Glasgow folk cross over here, but a much greater number to visit the birthplace of parents or grandparents. The accents of Clydeside seem strange on the lips of the first cousin of an O'Boyle or a Murphy, a Whiteford, O'Neill or O'Kane, but our Scottish friends appear to enjoy themselves during their stay and some of the girls even accept the invitation to change their names and become permanent residents here – thus counterbalancing the number of local girls who marry Glaswegians.

The Green Point district of Brooklyn, New York, is another spot where Glensfolk have congregated within the past couple of generations and they have founded a County Antrim Association there.

A 'greenhorn' Glensman is always welcomed and if necessary helped to find his feet in the New World, and in the case of the Irish-American who has been able to pay a visit to the

'Old Country' his return to the land of his adoption is usually marked by an informal celebration, where he is besieged by people anxious for first-hand news from 'home'.

They tell the story of one such ex-patriate who was approached by an embarrassed-looking young man:

'Say, Tom,' he began, 'did you see that goil Nora — , Peter's daughter when you were in the Glens?'

'I sure did!' said the chap addressed, heartily. 'Why?'

'Wal, I was a bit sweet on her back home, an' I wrote a few letters to her, but now I've fallen for another dame. I'd be tickled to death to hear she'd got another guy.'

'Don't worry, son,' said the other, 'come over here and meet the wife' – and who was she but the former Nora — !

Whether or not he was 'tickled to death' has not been recorded. One thing is certain, however – of the girls who went to the United States or Canada in the emigration times, very few remained single for long!

Nine Glens folk have the name of being very clannish, a trait that is best illustrated by the following true story.

During the pre-war years many coasters from all over the UK congregated at St Malo, the port in north-west France, awaiting the early new potato cargoes (the 'Spud Run') which went to Southampton, Liverpool, Newcastle, etc. On this occasion unseasonable weather had held up the digging, and for a week St Malo had become a port where more English dialects than French were heard.

One evening while we were in a café, some of the Frenchmen present got into an argument with a few of the sailors off another ship. In such cases, where there seemed no disparity in numbers, we didn't do more than see fair play, but the row wasn't on two minutes till one of the sailors shouted, 'Up Ballyeamon!' as he sailed into a burly 'Froggy'. Instantly two of our chaps (as it seemed instinctively) rose and entered the fray, their reinforcement causing a French rout. When we asked them afterwards (one was a fireman from Glenarm, the other a deck hand from Carnlough) they admitted that they had never seen the Ballyeamon man before – nor had either of them set foot in Ballyeamon in his life!

Leffmesse

The word 'Lammas' is derived from the Old Saxon word 'Leffmesse' and was in olden times the day when the first fruits of the corn, i.e. loaves, were given in thanksofferings. Lammas was also a period of thanksgiving and celebration in Ireland, even in pagan times, many 'aenachs' or fairs being held all over the country. Tailteann, in County Meath, for instance, had a yearly fair which was held on the days preceding, including and following August 1. Dating from 200 BC, it was devoted to games, trials of skill between noted warriors and athletes, contests between bards, with a very important section where marriages were performed.

Dunmaul, which crowns Garron Head, was also the scene of an old-time aenach, as was Cargan, but the only survivor of these events in Co. Antrim is the Lammas Fair of Ballycastle.

The Lammas Fair

The Lammas Fair, now held each year on the last Tuesday of August, bore more resemblance to the ancient aenach than any of its contemporaries. It was the annual hosting of the MacDonnells – and McDonalds – when the Antrim Scots met the Scots in Antrim, and in those early times was a three-day affair.

Red-shanked Highlanders, resplendent in new holiday kilt and plaid, the distinctive clan tartan showing at its best, silver breast-pin and polished sporran gleaming in the sunlight, caught the eye of many a Scots-Irish cailin, and numerous romances dated from the Lammas Fair.

Games of 'shinty' were played (the forerunner of modern hurling, but still called shinty in Scotland), and trials of strength and skill were held as in the Highland Games, now an annual event at Balmoral, Aberdeenshire.

Calgary, Alberta, has its Highland Games where descendants of the Scottish settlers in that part of Canada carry on the old traditions, tossing the caber and shinty being popular diversions.

In the Ballycastle event there was a mixture of the Scottish and the Irish, especially as regards music. The skirl of the pipes could be heard, a Highlander playing for his Antrim kinsmen the latest strathspey, reel or lament; in a chieftain's abode the sweet notes of a harp entertained his visitors as they feasted, while on the streets the business of dealing in cattle and highland ponies was briskly carried on.

The scene at night was a gay one, with groups of dancers revolving in the intricacies of jig or reel, the while the older spectators applauded their efforts to tire each other down. The only light was from torches of pitch-pine, or bonfires before which on huge spits roasted whole sides of oxen that were maybe an O'Cahan's until a week before. Perhaps, too, the enmities were laid aside during aenach time and the penalty for unprovoked aggression was death to the aggressor.

Nowadays, even if shorn of much of its former glory, the

Lammas Fair is most interesting as the only survival in Ulster of these events.

There is still a considerable amount of business done, especially in sheep, and thousands of sight-seeing visitors throng the town in addition to shepherds, farmers and dealers.

'Dulse' and 'Yella-man' (a kind of yellowish candy or drawn toffee) with 'hard nuts' (a cross between a rock cake and biscuit, and ranging from walnut size to about twice that) were eagerly-bought commodities for which the Fair was famous. It was no unusual spectacle to see a cross-Channel visitor, man or woman, popular politician or famous film star, munching (and enjoying) these delicacies from a paper bag!

That was one of the greatest attractions of the event; there was a go-as-you-please, informal air about the whole gathering that put everybody at ease. There was no regimentation of amusement – in fact you were encouraged to supply your own – and even the buskers did not seem to be doing their stuff solely for what money it brought them!

That was one of the greatest attractions for hearing a representative selection of Nine Glens' dialects. You can hear somebody talking about 'splitting the differs', or 'giein' a luck-penny' in a bit of bargaining; you can hear somebody described as 'whitely-faced', or 'dark-avised', or even as a 'wee, unsignified crathur'. A customer in a tobacconist's can be heard saying that he wants an ounce to smoke now and 'twa oonces t' pit in the spleuchan (pouch) for again' (i.e. for later on). If the booze is anyway plentiful, you'll hear of the chap who had a 'prakus' of it (which is next door to a skinful!) and so on.

There are ballad singers galore and anyone interested in this branch of folklore can hear ballads which are well worth collecting and which may not perhaps be sung anywhere else. Where these songsters come from, and where they go the rest of the year, is a mystery, but I know that ballads of which only fragments had previously been collected have been heard sung in full in Ballycastle, on the last Tuesday of August.

The Oul' Lammas Fair of Ballycastle, written by the late John H. McAuley, who kept a little bog-oak souvenir shop in Ann Street, was an instantaneous hit from the day it was published, and visitors to Ballycastle came away humming its catchy air. Like all true ballads, it wastes no time in preliminary flights of fancy.

At the Ould Lammas Fair in Ballycastle long ago,
I met a little colleen who set my heart aglow;
She was smiling at her daddy buying lambs from Paddy Roe,
At the Ould Lammas Fair of Ballycastle O!
I seen her home that night when the moon was shining bright,
From the Ould Lammas Fair of Ballycastle O!

Bustling Ballycastle

Ballycastle is one of the most go-ahead seaside resorts on the Antrim Coast, ranking in this respect second only to Portrush. Its history is inextricably linked up with that of the clan Donnell and any account of Ballycastle must begin with a reference to the McDonnells, whose monuments are strewn in every burying-ground from Glenshesk to Glenarm – and some few also who lie in unmarked graves among the heather.

Outstanding among the McDonnells was 'Sorley Boy', who, when offered a grant of lands that he gained by the sword, answered Queen Elizabeth's offer in these words: 'What I have won with the sword I will keep with the sword!' And keep it he did, despite many efforts to dislodge him.

Near Ballycastle is laid the scene of two of the most beautiful tales in Ireland's rich storehouse, *The Children of Lir* and *The fate of Deirdre and the Sons of Uisneach*. We have already heard the tale of *The Children of Lir*, for Cushendall people hold that it was in a little natural harbour at the foot of the river Dall that Finola and her brothers sheltered and we can now learn what befell poor Deirdre as told in one of the *Tales of Ancient Erin*, and translated by Eugene O'Curry, *The Fate of Deirdre and the Sons of Uisneach*.

The Fate of Deirdre and the Sons of Uisneach

According to this, about the first century AD, Conor was King of Ulster, his palace being at Emania (Navan Fort, near Armagh). When a girl-child called Deirdre was born it was predicted that she should be the cause of the ruin of the Kingdom of Ulster, but Conor, despite this, took her under his care and had her reared in his own household, his intention being to take her to wife when old enough.

Deirdre, with the usual unpredictability of women, upset this arrangement badly by falling in love with Naisi, one of the sons of Uisneach, and persuading him to fly with her to Scotland. His two brothers accompanied them and they spent a couple of happy years in the vicinity of Loch Etive, Argyllshire.

During their absence a grand banquet was given in Emania by King Conor, at which all the Chieftains of Ulster were present. During this feast Conor was so mellowed by the happiness and friendship visible on every face that he decided to grant the first reasonable request his guests might make.

'Know you of any want under which you lie?' he asked.

There was a short consultation, then a spokesman answered, 'It is a pity, O Conor, that the sons of Uisneach should fall in an enemy land, for they are great in valour and prowess.'

This request was the most distasteful that could have been put to him, and Conor tried to back down by reminding the chiefs that the sons of Uisneach were under a solemn vow not to return unless with, and under the protection of, Fergus McRiogh, Conal Cearach or Cuchulainn, Ulster's three greatest champions.

'Then let one of those three be despatched to Alba,' (Scotland) was the answer.

Unwillingly the king gave way. Choosing Fergus McRiogh as their escort, Conor put him under a vow, which Fergus was to impose also upon the sons of Uisneach, not to halt when they set foot in Erin, but to come at once to Emania, and not to break their fast from when they landed until they took their first meal at the royal palace.

Fergus set out to escort the three heroes and Deirdre on their homeward journey and in the meantime Conor got one of his courtiers, Barach (whose 'dun' or castle was near where they expected to land) to prepare a banquet for them.

When the five landed, Deirdre, with a premonition of tragedy, turned and gazed sadly back at Alba, saying, 'My love to you, O land yonder in the East.'

Barach, to cause them to break their vow, offered them a meal, with every protestation of friendship.

Fergus, seeing the trap, was full of indignation, but Deirdre tried to persuade her husband and the other two that the best plan was to let Fergus settle with Barach while they sought refuge in Rathlin.

The sons of Uisneach weren't the type to take such advice, so they pushed on for Emania, where Conor got some of his foreign mercenaries to attack them (none of the native chiefs would have anything to do with the crime).

After a tremendous struggle, minutely described in the 'Tale', the three heroes were slain.

Fergus McRiogh, disgusted and full of hostility to the treacherous king, went into voluntary exile in Connacht, and later he was guide and director of the military expedition of the Connacht men against Conor.

Cormac Conloingeas, who was a son of Conor, also voluntarily exiled himself for the same reason.

This crime, said to have been the first case in Ireland's history of treachery on the part of a ruler – did not profit Conor much, as it was eventually the cause of the revolt of the chieftains that led to his being deposed from the kingship.

Carrig-Uisneach is where the repatriates landed and where the present Torr Head look-out station stands is supposed to have been the site of the home of Barach, whose burial-place is in the vicinity.

Place-Names are Potted Stories

One of the things which make our country so attractive to the visitor is the way we have of perpetuating history in our names of places. A knowledge of Irish is, of course, a great advantage in understanding these names and the allusions they are meant to convey, so it would be a good idea for any places catering for visitors to publish a little brochure giving the translation of local place names, together with any folk-tales concerning them.

The neighbourhood of Ballycastle is exceptionally rich in place-names that are both musical and – to anyone who knows Irish – suggestive of romance or tragedy or both. Carrig-

Uisneach is only one example, but it is enough to stimulate curiosity regarding the intriguing names that occur so frequently.

Bun-na-Margy

The visitor to Ballycastle is advised (as guide books say) to see the ancient Bun-na-Margy Abbey, one of the most history-steeped ruins in Ireland, the burial-place of the McQuillans and later of the McDonnells, and the scene, despite its ecclesiastical associations, of many a stern struggle between warriors during our country's troubled history.

It was at Bun-na-Margy, too, that Julia McQuillan, the famous 'Black Nun', had her hermit's cell and the story is told that when her sister who, like Magdalen, had sinned, came to visit her, Julia refused her admittance.

Not a very saintly act that, you'll say!

No, but when she had repulsed the weeping woman her conscience troubled her, the more so when (so the story goes) a blackbird on a nearby bush piped, 'Let her in! Let her in!' Looking through the narrow window of her hermitage she beheld her sister on her knees, her hands raised in supplication to her Heavenly Father, while a strange unearthly light hovered over her face, upon which had descended a quiet peace.

Then did Julia realise that where God had granted forgiveness she had greatly erred in withholding hers, so she emerged from her retreat and approached her sister – too late, alas! – for death had claimed her.

Many local traditions are current extolling the virtues and penances of Julia, who is also said to have had the gift of prophecy.

As befits a place whose precincts have been a burial-ground for their ancestor for about six hundred years, the people of

Ballycastle and district hold Bun-na-Margy in great veneration.

Founded somewhere about the 14th century, most likely by the then ruling family in North Antrim, the McQuillans, it was a Franciscan Abbey right down through their internecine warfare with the McDonnells and the successful campaign of Shane O'Neill in 1565, when some of his men were billeted there.

It seems to have been splendid type of building for its period of erection and even yet, with its roofless walls open to the sky, it retains a certain rare dignity. It is now one of the ruins under the protection of the Ministry of Home Affairs, in conjunction with the Archaeological Section of the Belfast Naturalist Society.

Randal, first Marquis of Antrim (whose history was given during our visit to Glenarm) was buried in Bun-na-Margy, with three inscriptions on his leaden coffin. The one in Irish has been translated as follows: 'At all times some calamity befalls the Irish every seventh year, but now that the Marquis is departed it will occur every year.' The inscription in Latin records his loyalty to 'Country, Charles and God' (the order of precedence seems to have been a bit confused!) then goes on to say, 'Thyself a golden warrior, thou residest within the lead, whose fidelity in the adverse fortune of war, rebels nor gibbets could not bend.'

Our First Coal Mine
What is supposed to have been one of the first coal mines worked anywhere in these islands is that now called the 'North Star'. When miners were driving fresh galleries during the development of the district under Mr Hugh Boyd's lease from the Earl of Antrim in 1770, they broke through into a series of old workings, the tools in which showed that they had been operated by coal-hewers of long, long ago. It has even been

suggested that they may have been Phoenicians, who had such a keen nose for valuable minerals, and were the pioneers of tin-mining in Cornwall.

For a time Ballycastle looked like becoming one of the foremost industrial towns in Ireland, when the above-mentioned Hugh Boyd established collieries, tanneries, iron foundries, salt-pans, a brewery and even a glass-works. Parliament voted £23,000 to construct a harbour, but after Boyd's death the tide of prosperity receded and Ballycastle seemed on the road to decay – another 'deserted village' in fact.

All credit to its inhabitants for their struggle to prevent this. Seeing the hopelessness of trying to retain their industrial position, they concentrated upon the attracting of tourists. Tourism in those early days depended for its increase upon the personal recommendation of people who had visited a resort, rather a slow, if sure, method of expansion, but the hoteliers of Ballycastle were quick to see the value of advertising, and by means of attractive brochures, newspaper space and posters they made the health-giving and beautiful features of the village and district known to thousands.

6

A Grand Panorama

We now come to the last of the Glens on our tour, Glenshesk, four miles from Ballycastle and one that has more traditions of ancient warfare than any other, situated as it was at the nearest point to the part of Scotland whence came the Northmen in their forays, and in later days whence the Hebridean clansmen descended upon the Antrim McQuillans and O'Cahans.

The final contact between McDonnell and McQuillan was on the slopes of Aura, but the earlier battles, in which McQuillan was victorious, were fought up and down the valley of Glenshesk. Almost every field or enclosure there has its story of an encounter, the district is studded with the graves of warriors who fell with weapons bared, and to this day occasional finds are made of dirks, swords or skeans-dhu used in the conflict.

Let us stand at the head of Glenshesk and view the scene: Away on the right is the curving point of 'Benmore' or Fair Head. It rises in sullen grandeur from the sea, a steep precipice towering over the debris of some of its fallen columns, the waves on a wild day showing white spray and spindrift as they dash themselves impotently against it. To westward is Kenbane or Kenbaan Head, as white as Benmore is dark, with its many-fissured limestone cliffs, and the background is filled by Knocklayde, rising to 1,695 feet. This slope, heather-clad to its summit, must have often reminded the Scots of the purple-heather hills of their native Highlands.

The isle of Rathlin, with a stretch of swift tidal water between it and the mainland, looks like some huge amphibian basking in the sunlight, and away in the far distance are visible Islay, the Paps of Jura, Cantyre, Sanda Island, Ailsa Craig ('Paddy's Milestone'), and behind it a dim glimpse of the coast of Ayrshire – a wonderful panorama.

Guglielmo Marconi carried out some of his early experiments from Ballycastle to Rathlin, and the Rathlin-Ballycastle wireless station, opened on January 1, 1901, was the first to be established in the United Kingdom, the radio telephone system being installed in 1935.

Kenbaan Head
The castle on Kenbaan Head was another McDonnell eyrie, its last occupant being Randal McAllister. A daughter of McAllister, Rose, married Hugh Boyd, the benevolent founder of so many Ballycastle industries.

This whole district is dotted with the earthen ramparts that mark where 'duns' existed from pre-Christian times down to the evolution of the all-stone fort. The local traditions attached to these ancient raths or duns would take too long to tell here, but Dunraine, 'Fort of the Queen'; Dun-a-Mallaght, 'Fort of the Curse', Duncarbit and farther inland the well-preserved site of Dunbought, Dungonnell, Dunaghy and many more are reminders that this corner of Antrim played an important part in our ancient history.

The Grey Man's Path

Although Fair Head looks from here to be one huge mass, when we reach its summit we find that the hand of Nature has divided it by an awe-inspiring chasm. It is possible to descend to the foot of the twin precipices that enclose it and from there to have an unforgettable view of it, the huge pillar that has fallen across and bridged it seeming like the work of some giant architect or engineer.

Nobody seems to know who this 'Grey Man' was, the user – or maker – of this path, but he was certainly one who believed in doing things on a grand scale! If you want to realise how puny man really is, stand on this path and look upwards, and even the knowledge that you can split the atom won't make you feel 'big'!

James Studdert Moore has expressed the local feeling regarding the 'Grey Man' in his poem, *The Grey Man's Path*, from which the following is an extract:

> A pillared chasm, rude and stern,
> Cleft by the hand of God,
> From whose high arch of stone the tern
> And seamew sweep abroad.
>
> 'Tis there, at midnight's silent hour,
> The mystic Grey Man glides
> Along the tops of rugged rocks,
> Or down their sloping sides.
>
> From far below, like a wail of woe,
> From caves where otters sleep,
> Comes booming along a mystic song,
> Paean of the mighty deep.

Each good ship steers for the ocean wide,
Away from Bengore Head,
And comes not near that rocky shore
Till the fatal hour is sped.

For the ship that nears that ghostly form
Shall wrecked and riven lie,
While the mangled forms of her hapless crew
Shall strew the shore hard by.

And woe betide the peasant lone
Who meets him on the shore,
For he shall see his cottage home
Or family nevermore.

Carrick-a-Rede

Another place where you suddenly lose your self-importance is at
Carrick-a-Rede, five miles along the upper coast from Ballycastle.
Here is situated the famous 'Swinging Bridge' which stretches
from the mainland to a small island. This bridge, which is at each
end about 90 feet above sea level, is constructed of two cables
made fast to iron rings firmly fixed in the rock, with cross-
lashings, planks being laid on top of these. There are also two
hand-ropes, whose support is more psychological than real.

Get on to the bridge (it sags in the middle, remember) when
there is a bit of a breeze blowing and it is swaying about, and if
you were seeking a thrill – you've had it!

The fishermen use this, the only means of communication,
during the fishing season, March–October, and people who
graze sheep there carry the animals to and from it with

completed nonchalance. It is worthwhile going to see the sheep migration even if you don't cross the contraption yourself!

The view from Sheep Island is somewhat unique, and you can easily picture yourself as marooned on an inaccessible spur, this illusion, if it might be called, being heightened if there happens to be a bit of fog and you cannot see the mainland.

Nature in the Raw

The Rev. William Hamilton, DD, FTCD, MRIA, published in 1786 a book called *Letters Concerning the Northern Coast of the County of Antrim*, in which he dealt with, among other things, the geology of the district. He had plenty of material to draw from, for this certainly resembles a countryside where volcanoes had played havoc long ago, and geologists tell us that the black rocks fringing County Antrim are of volcanic origin.

Imagine our seacoast to be completely denuded of its vegetation, with rocks standing up like huge nightmare figures in suspended animation, and there you have a picture of Antrim after the volcanoes had finished with it. Such a scene is common in Iceland within a few miles of where villages have been established, as Iceland's volcanoes were active until comparatively recently (one or two erupt a little even today).

A visit to one of these Icelandic collections of natural statuary is like seeing your worst nightmare embodied in stone. There are satyrs, gargoyles, Medusa's heads and other figures that look like exaggerations of Epstein's most extravagant flights of fancy. At one period in the evolution of our country we had similar figures but the hand of time has softened their wildest contours and in some cases clothed their indecency with a mantle of earth and verdure.

The geologist is certain to find there a most fruitful field for study, as our strata are exposed in a way that to him must be a composite picture of old Mother Earth's progress from atomic chaos to present-day chaotic atom-splitting. All the intervening ages have left their deposits, from the Palaeozoic or primary epoch down through the Mesozoic with its subdivisions into Triassic, Jurassic and Cretaceous systems, the Cainozoic, and the Post-Tertiary or more recent geological divisions.

Cushendun Caves, for instance, consist of what is virtually a one-time section of the sea bed, containing an immense number of specimens of fossilized marine creatures and dotted like a well-fruited plum cake with stones of almost every known kind, the only place comparable with it being the famous Gem Grotto near Fowey, Cornwall, where precious and semi-precious stones have been collected from all over the world and cemented into its walls.

Stages in Evolution

Our Nine Glens, and the numerous smaller valleys near them, were scooped out by a giant, so the story goes. True enough, but the 'giant' was the huge ice-sheet that drifted with slow but irresistible force from the north during the transition from the glacial to a warmer epoch.

We know that when the warmer age caused the ice to melt, the country gradually assumed the appearance of a vast forest, the only bare part being a narrow belt contiguous to the coast. From the numerous 'kitchen middens' found there we can deduce that the first human beings landed at or near Whitepark Bay, whence they followed the coastline, subsisting upon shell-fish and any other fish they could catch, their primitive weapons serving only rarely to kill the larger edible animals. Traces of the now extinct auk, a large swimming bird, have also been found.

Later, as they improved their weapons and devised ways of trapping, their diet included flesh such as that of the elk. When they began to forsake the nomadic and embrace a pastoral way of life, they invented tools to clear the forests, and supply pasture for the animals they had domesticated. They were of necessity compelled to remain to a certain extent nomadic even then, until the discovery that tilling the soil could produce an abundance both of fodder and food for themselves allowed them to peg down in one spot – and so agriculture was born.

On March 22, 1946, a well-preserved skeleton belonging to this, the Early Bronze Age of mankind, was found on the farm of Mr Charles Monaghan, Foriff, Glenariff. The discovery was quite accidental: Monaghan was building up a sod ditch with the soil near it and in doing so his spade struck a stone. Fearing that this stone might interfere with his ploughing later on, he started to dig round it so as to remove it, and was surprised to find that it was a large limestone slab over four feet long. With the assistance of his brother and a neighbour it was turned over and a cist was exposed, lined with other small slabs. Their curiosity aroused, they dug into the sand which filled the cist, and shortly came upon the skeleton in a posture which suggested that it had been buried on its side with the knees drawn up to the chin. Beside it was an urn, bearing an incised decoration round the upper part. This urn was about six inches in height, about the same in diameter, and had a couple of protuberances about two inches down on the outside, each having a hole through it about a quarter-inch diameter. Unfortunately, the urn got broken through one of the spades striking it, but its reconstruction was an easy task, and later examination of the site by Professor Walmsley of the Department of Anatomy, Queen's University, Belfast, resulted in many interesting facts coming to light about this burial place of one of our earliest ancestors.

It appeared, from certain characteristics of the skeleton, notably a flattening of the tibia (shinbone) and fibula, that it belonged to a race whose presence at one time in Ireland was only discovered about 1928, when several graves of the same type were found at Ballymoney, County Antrim, and a few others in County Derry. These people, according to Professor Walmsley, left Persia about 1500 BC, made their way up the Danube and across Europe, established themselves for some time in Norfolk, a few pushing up north as far as Scotland.

The finding of this skeleton seems to settle the point as to where they landed in Ireland, as its proximity to the former sea beach seems to show that they had a stronghold at Red Bay after landing there. Another interesting fact is that the type of cist-burial proved that it was a chieftain whose remains were found, as a cruder type of interment sufficed for the ordinary rank and file. These class distinctions!

Ours must have been a wild land in those days, with many volcanoes still showing periodic activity and large and ferocious animals, such as bears, roaming the forests, not to mention the packs of wolves. (The wild cat, a prehistoric animal, survives in some of the more inaccessible parts of north Scotland even today.)

Mention of volcanoes recalls an attempt to build up a most sensational story about an eruption of Knocklayde as recently as May, 1788, in which it was alleged that a village called Ballyowen was turned into a miniature Pompeii by a huge stream of lava which engulfed it.

A Lie-vely Volcano

The origin of the story seems to have been an extract from a letter, supposed to have come from Ballycastle, which appeared in the *Dublin Chronicle* of June 7, 1788.

The gave what was apparently an 'accurate account' of the volcanic eruption and earthquake: 'Preceded by a noise resembling a continued crash of thunder, a huge column of fire and smoke burst forth and ascended about 60 yards into the air, followed by a shower of ashes and stones which extended a quarter of a mile round the hill. In about 46 minutes after the first shock a stream of lava poured out and rushed in a sheet of liquid fire about 60 yards in breadth down the fields until it entered the adjoining village of Ballyowen, where it involved the houses and their unfortunate inhabitants in conflagration and ruin, none having escaped but one man, his wife and two children; and after the lava had continued to flow for about 39 hours it then totally ceased.'

The Glensman, a regrettably short-lived but most interesting little monthly, whose owner-editor was Mr G.B. New, Cushendall, had a reference to this 'eruption' in its edition for January, 1932, in which mention was made of an article in the *Northern Whig* of December 23, 1931. This article, by 'North Antrim', showed that the story of the Knocklayde eruption was 'an eighteenth century invention' and the reason why the tale is repeated is to warn readers who may come across it in Connellan's edition of *The Annals of the Four Masters* or Seward's *Topography of Ireland*. Both Connellan and Seward apparently believed the yarn, though it did not deceive Dr Hamilton, who makes no reference to it in the second edition of his *Letters*, published in 1790.

Pompeii was destroyed in AD 79, and its site was discovered in 1748, but it seems unlikely that an antiquarian excavator will in AD 3457 come upon the ruins or remains of Ballyowen!

Brecan's Pot

Before we visit Rathlin, we may learn a little about the whirlpool that exists off its coast. The tide runs very strongly between Ballycastle and the Island, the channel between Rathlin and the Mull of Kintyre having also a rather swift run. When these two come together, at the south end of the island, a whirlpool is created, called in the native language 'Corrievrechan' or 'Brecan's Pot', a miniature edition of the maelstrom (the huge whirlpool situated south of the Lofoten Islands, north-west coast of Norway).

The Rathlin whirlpool may be only small in comparison, but it could be extremely dangerous for a small boat coming within range of its pull. You have often seen, when the bath-plug is withdrawn, the whirlpool careering madly round the entrance to the wastepipe. Well, that gives a fairly good idea of the shape of Corrievrechan when in angry mood.

To the small, light boats used in ancient times, such a whirlpool must have constituted a real danger. An old manuscript (*Cormac's Glossary*) written about 900 AD, and translated by Dr Reeves, tells of Brecan, a grandson of Niall of the Nine Hostages, whose fifty curraghs, while trading between Eire and Alba (Ireland and Scotland) were drawn into the 'cauldron' and engulfed without a survivor.

No wonder it had a bad name among succeeding generations of seafarers!

Visit to Rathlin

As the weather seems in a good mood today, we'll board the motor-boat at the little pier and take a look at Rathlin. A notice says: 'Leaving at 10.30 a.m. on Mondays, Wednesdays and Fridays (weather permitting)' and as we seat ourselves we sincerely hope that weather will remain permissive enough to make our return trip as comfortable as the outward one.

There are a few of the inhabitants down to see the boat arrive, people who bear a startling resemblance to the natives of the islands of the Hebrides. Take any half-dozen Rathliners, men and women, put them on Islay, Tyree, Barra or Skye, and I defy anyone to pick them out as 'foreigners' without applying the language test (the Hebrideans all have the Scots Gaelic as well as English).

This is not hard to explain: most of the Rathlin folk came there from the coast of North Antrim, most of the people on the North Antrim coast are descended from the Scots, McDonnells, McNeills, McCouags (or McQuigg), Ogilvies and such with a Darragh or O'Cahan (O'Kane) to give the leavening of the original Irish stock. On the other hand, the Hebrideans in the old days often visited the coast from Bundoran to Ballycastle, fishing or dealing, and many of them took Irish wives back with them.

Rathlin is about five miles long, is shaped like an Australian boomerang, with ends pointing towards the mainland, and is a mile broad. It was well known to ancient navigators, and was mentioned as Ricina by both Pliny and Ptolemy.

Its prominent position at the entrance to the Sea of Moyle, and its proximity to the coast of Ireland made it a target for the Danish corsairs, who attacked it on many occasions mostly with little success, though in the year 790 they destroyed its monastery, founded during the lifetime of St Columba of the Churches (St Columbkille, 521–587).

Bruce's Castle

The story of Robert Bruce and the spider is too well-known to repeat here, as the lesson taught him, when he sought shelter on Rathlin after his defeat in 1306 at Perth, and witnessed the six attempts of the little animal to reach its objective, culminating in a successful seventh essay, has been pointed out to many generations of schoolboys since.

The place where this paragon of perseverance played its part in reanimating Robert's courage is supposed to have been 'Bruce's Castle' of which little more than the foundation remains, and there is also a 'Bruce's Cave', another hideout of his.

Rathlin was the place to which the Scots retreated when things got too hot for them on the Irish mainland, but it must have been an awful experience for the McDonnell chieftain, Sorley Boy, when he had to stand impotent on the shore of Ballycastle and see his people, including his own wife and family, being hunted and mercilessly butchered.

Inter-clan Massacres

This happened in 1575, when a force under Captain John Norris (or Norreys) landed on the island while Sorley was absent and put almost everyone there to the sword, completing the job by razing most of the dwelling-places.

Rathlin was, in April 1642, the scene of another massacre, when the men were all killed and most of the women thrown over the cliffs at a place still called Port-na-Calliagh. Two other names which commemorate this massacre are Lagnavistavor, 'the hollow of defeat', and Crookascreidlin, 'the hill of screaming', where the women and children stood watching the menfolk dying in defence of family and home, and many of the women realised that their own fate hung upon the outcome of the unequal struggle.

In Hill's *McDonnells of Antrim*, the story is told of one woman who was not killed by the fall but was later discovered by a Campbell to be still alive. He gave her what aid he could, then had her brought to his own home in the Rhynns of Islay, where she recovered. Her former husband had been killed before her eyes during the massacre, and her only child, a son, had disappeared, so when Campbell asked her to be his wife she consented.

Many years afterwards she felt an irresistible urge to revisit the scenes of her youth, and when she had landed on Rathlin and made for where her first married years had been spent, she was overjoyed to find that her son had escaped and was in possession of what had been his father's little farm.

The perpetrators of this horrible deed were 1,600 Campbells under Sir Duncan Campbell of Auchinbreck, and even yet the islanders look askance at anyone bearing the unhallowed name of Campbell.

Cuchulainn on Rathlin

In one of the Irish tales called 'Tochmarc Eimhire', Cuchulainn was returning from a renowned military school in Scotland (where he had been perfecting his knowledge of the warlike arts) when he landed on Rathlin.

Here he was surprised to find a beautiful young lady sitting alone on the shore and was even more amazed to find that she was the Island King's daughter, whom the Fomorian pirates were forcing her father to hand over to them in place of the annual tribute they had exacted, and which he had been unable to gather that year.

As she related her doleful tale a boat landed three of the fiercest of the pirates, who came confidently up to the appointed rendezvous.

Cuchulainn awaited their coming, and instead of their lovely prize they found a well-armed champion barring their way. A hot encounter ensued, in which Cuchulainn killed all three of them, his only wound being a deep scratch on one arm which the girl bandaged with a bit torn off her rich robe.

She then ran off to tell her father, who had been sadly bewailing her loss, of her deliverance. He joyfully informed his people and also some visitors to his Court, but the girl was unable to describe her rescuer minutely enough for him to be identified, though it was believed he was still on the island.

A celebration was arranged to which all the courtiers and the visitors were invited, and as was customary the King led the guests to where the ablutions prior to a feast were performed.

On the way a few members of the entourage began to hint that they had been the girl's champion, but when Cuchulainn removed his cloak she saw and recognised the bandage on his arm.

The king was delighted with the handsome, modest hero, and with the full concurrence of his daughter offered Cuchulainn her hand and fortune.

It somewhat spoils the story to have to tell that Cuchulainn was compelled to refuse this very generous offer because he was already engaged to the lovely Eimer (for whose sake he had encountered as many perils as Jason did when seeking the Golden Fleece) and whom he eventually married.

Life on Rathlin

Winter in Rathlin might be regarded as unbearable and dull by anyone accustomed to town life, or even country-dwellers used to more spacious areas, but the Rathliners seem to be able to enjoy the indoor season quite well.

They are fond of dancing, and hold regular ceilidthe, at which (as was the original ceilidthe custom) both young and old attend, and when you see the happy couples moving through the intricacies of a 'Waves of Tory' or 'set' of quadrilles dance you begin to realise that most of our modern syncopated swingers have missed something, while the pleased faces of the older folk prove that enjoyment of such dancing is not confined solely to the dancers themselves.

Compare the face of a mother watching her daughter dancing in a reel, hornpipe or schottische with that of a mother viewing her daughter's gyrations in a spot of 'jitterbugging' and you'll get the idea!

Moira O'Neill's poem, *The Rachray Man*, describes the islanders as 'rightin' and tearin' away', which was an undeserved slur upon a place where there is only one pub, no policeman and where the people live in great amity.

(There may be a bit of a scrap between two rivals for a local beauty's favour, but you don't have to travel all the way to Rathlin to see that!)

Lovely Lassies

It may be mentioned in this connection that the number of

beauties among Rathlin girls is proportionately great. Whether it is due to the air, the food, the water or not too many late nights, they have complexions that beat anything the face-lifters can produce.

It is amusing to see the envious glances of the fair visitors upon whom the 'beauty expert' has exercised her greatest skill, as they realise that nature is still the paramount beautifier!

Like all withdrawn communities, Rathlin has various superstitions. The lough Ashet has a kelpie or water-sprite who in the old days was in the habit of enticing young people to its edge, then dragging them beneath the water.

There is a firm belief in overlooking or 'blinking' as it is called. Certain persons are credited with the power of bringing evil upon anyone whom they envy or dislike, so that cattle die or refuse to give milk, horses drop in harness and hens stop laying. Such powers are, of course, derived from the devil, with whom the evil-eyed person is in league!

Fairies are reputed to have at one time inhabited the various mounds dotted here and there over the island, and numerous stories tell of the benevolent and malevolent acts of the wee folk. The grogah is, as usually, very prominent in these yarns, and the old tale of the leprechaun and the crock of gold is repeated with many embellishments and variations.

'Ghost' yarns are not popular, doubtless owing to the fact that nobody cares to listen to these at a neighbour's fireside and then tramp home at a late hour along a lonely moorland path, feeling his scalp grow taut at every unwonted sound – or even at the eerie quietude – and jumping if he sights a sheep's white fleece through the darkness. Another factor which contributes to this dislike of ghost yarns is the knowledge that one can hardly tread upon a foot of Rathlin ground without stepping upon a place where some of the victim of the massacres 'Wel-tered in theer Gore' — as the Thespians used to declaim in the old full-blooded or full-of-blood dramas of last century.

Rathlin has many remains of old subterranean chambers, souterrains they are called, the purpose of which can only be guessed. Some antiquaries believe that they were the dwelling places of a small race of people who antedated the Celts; others hold that they were constructed as temporary hiding places during the periodic invasions of the Norsemen.

One thing is certain; no people of average present-day stature could have lived in any sort of comfort in dwellings whose roof never exceeds 4 feet in height.

This drawback does not altogether rule them out as temporary hiding places, but the writer is inclined to believe that these souterrains were the homes of the small people who came to be mentioned in the folklore of their conquerors as the 'fairies' or by the more accurate title, 'wee people'.

When St Patrick banished the snakes from Ireland he must have included Rathlin, as no snakes or other poisonous reptiles are found there, though in the Scottish islands the common adder, viper verus, is to be found. This cannot be explained by the distance from Cantyre, as some of the Hebridean islands, such as Lewis, are farther from the Scottish mainland than is Rathlin to Ireland's.

This fact was adduced as proof of Rathlin's allegiance to Ireland, when some of the Scottish clans laid claim to it.

7

Folklore of the Glens

So far in our tour we have only made passing reference to the folklore of the Glens. As it is a most fascinating subject, let us now examine it in greater detail, though it would require a good-sized volume to give a collection of our folk-tales alone.

When the ancient faith was supplanted by Christianity it was found that the people clung to many of the superstitions of Druidism. Attempts to completely eradicate these failed, so the missionaries chose the line of least resistance and took a few harmless ones into the fold. Wells to which magic attributes had been ascribed – especially in the treatment of eye troubles – were blessed and henceforth became 'holy' wells; others whose water was used in baptising converts were regarded with respect in one generation and with veneration in the next.

(Analysis has proved that many such wells do contain elements that are beneficial when used in bathing the eyes.)

Cures, Charms and Folk-Tales

Other superstitions, though never at any time given Christian sanction, persisted not only in Ireland, England, Scotland and Wales, but, also under slightly differing forms all over Western Europe. France, Germany and the Baltic countries have their taboos – what we call 'freits' – such as the ill-luck attached to 13, or spilling salt, or meeting a red-haired woman first thing in the morning.

Some superstitious 'cures', such as those for whooping-cough – passing the child three times under a donkey's belly, or giving the youngster a piece of bread and jam which has been obtained from a woman who didn't change her surname at marriage (even Smith into Smythe or O'Cahan into Kane would do) – may seem nonsensical, but there are many who firmly believe in their efficacy.

Queer stories are related in the Glens of people who are reputed to possess a 'charm' against bleeding. Here is one about an occurrence early in the present century.

During quarrying operations on Glenariff a certain man was struck on the head by a falling stone. He received very severe injuries, and all the efforts of his mates could not staunch the haemorrhage, so that it seemed he must bleed to death, as the doctor was away from home.

Somebody recollected that a local man had the charm against bleeding so a messenger was sent post-haste to contact him. When found he was working, and when told of the accident he merely stood in silence for a moment or two, then turned away and seemed to murmur something.

The messenger grew impatient. 'Are you not coming?' he asked.

'No need,' said the charmer, 'the bleeding has stopped.'

The other man, incredulous, tried once more to get him to come with him.

'I tell you there's no need,' the charmer retorted angrily, as he picked up his spade again. 'Let me get on with my work!'

Disgusted at such seeming callousness, the messenger

remounted his bicycle and rode back expecting to find his workmate nearly dead.

What was his surprise, therefore, when he saw him sitting up, quite conscious, and not a drop of blood coming from any of his wounds!

It was later found that the cessation of the flow coincided with the messenger's delivery of the request for help to the man with the 'charm', so you may call it coincidence and let it go at that – but there are many other well-authenticated cases remembered by local folk.

'Second Sight'

The seventh son of a seventh son was popularly credited with the gift of 'second sight' and also with the power to cure certain diseases, mostly skin infections, by touching them with a wand of hazel. Nowadays, seventh sons are rare, not to speak of a duplication of that degree of fecundity, and it is as well, for these second-sighters must have been hard to live with!

Imagine walking along the road with one and when you met anyone, hearing him say of the passer-by, 'Poor Dan! I see his wraith is very close to him. He'll hardly last more than a week!'

Or fancy, if a girl, going for a walk with a seventh-of-seventh, and, just as he was about to try to kiss you (they do, you know!) your pretended surprise became alarm as he suddenly glanced over your shoulder and said, 'Mary, be very careful! I see you in your coffin over at that hedge there!'

Power of a Charm

I was told a most interesting story about the power of a charm, by a young Glensman whose grandfather figured in the tale.

In the old days it was common for a dealer in horses to engage a little Glens schooner to take him across to Scotland (usually Campbelltown) whence he went about gathering as many Highland ponies as made up a return cargo.

My informant's grandfather, besides being a farmer, was a horse-dealer and on this occasion took the vessel of which he was part owner to Campbelltown, whence he tramped the Kintyre peninsula, bringing in the horses he had purchased to where stabling was provided.

One of these was a very handsome grey, which he had obtained after much hard bargaining from an old woman living in a remote little croft he had never before visited.

Having at last got what he thought enough animals to show a worthwhile profit when resold at Cushendall Fair, he put them aboard and set sail for home.

A favouring wind sent them merrily along for a mile or two – then it suddenly swung half round the compass and, catching them unawares, almost dismasted them. They put about with enough to do and for two days lay at anchor while the animals ate all the fodder that was meant to last them to Red Bay.

A fresh stock of food and water, having been put aboard and the wind showing signs of veering, they weighed anchor and made another essay.

This time they had almost reached mid-channel before they were forced to return and again two days elapsed before the weather showed any sign of favouring them.

These days were very trying for the horses cooped up on board, many having come from where they had complete liberty on the moors, and the disgruntled dealer was giving them an inspection to see how they were faring, especially the grey (which he fancied for his own use), when something tied to her tail drew his attention.

Untying it, he walked over to the rail to examine it. It was a piece of some sort of plant, but adhering to it were three odd-looking things like little beans.

While puzzling out what purpose this queer tail-plait had served, he absent-mindedly flicked the wisp at the vessel's rail — and immediately there was a loud bang followed by another and another!

Naturally he was frightened, as were the members of the crew, but their fear was forgotten as they noticed that the wind had sprung up from the land and there was promise of a good passage.

They reached the home anchorage without further incident and set about landing their live cargo. All went well until the grey set foot upon the shore when it dropped dead in its tracks, dead as cats-meat!

Next time he was across the dealer sought out the old woman but all his searching failed to find either her or the house in which she had lived!

Drawing the Dew

May Day superstitions are legion. Be careful not to give even your best friend or neighbour a 'setting' of eggs on May 1, or your 'good luck' will be taken by the recipient. (Remember that in the old calendar New Year's Day was November 1, and midsummer May 1.)

Trailing a hair rope across a dewy field of grass on the morning of the 1st of May was supposed to have the effect of depriving that land of its fertility, and suspicion that an unfriendly neighbour had performed this rite has started many a long-lasting olden feud.

Another thing deemed unlucky was the expression – to the owner – of very high praise of one of his animals, such as a horse or a cow. It was believed that the beast thus lauded would shortly afterwards sicken and die, or meet with some fatal accident.

To the visitor who looked at a bonny baby and admiringly said, 'That's a lovely child,' it must have appeared very strange when the mother quickly snatched it up from its cradle and held it close at the same time turning her back on the innocent speaker – but such apparent rudeness was due to the maternal anxiety aroused when baby was praised without the addition of the evil-warding words, 'God bless it!'

Cutting the 'Cailleach'

There are some strange customs connected with harvest time, but none more so than Cutting the Cailleach.

If you happen to be passing a field where corn is being cut, you may notice the lads and lasses there engaged in what appears to be some frolic which causes a lot of shouting and laughter among them. If the corn is nearly all cut you are in luck, for you have happened upon the performance of an ancient rite, 'Cutting the Cailleach'.

In the old days people believed that a wee fairy woman called the Cailleach or Spirit of the Corn lived in the field from the time the first ears sprouted. They believed also that at cutting-time she darted from place to place in the crop until cornered in the last sheaf – but at that stage she was to be allowed to make for the shelter of the hedge before this last sheaf was cut.

In those days all the cutting was done with the sickle or reaping-hook, so the reapers stood off the last patch a bit, called out some particular incantation in Irish (now forgotten) and threw their hooks at it with a revolving motion.

Whoever cut the last of it was judged to be the person who drove the Cailleach out, and he got the best place at the harvest home dance that night.

As one old farmer told me when I asked him did anyone really believe the Cailleach was there, 'Oh, aye, the oul' people believed she was in it right enough, an' there's ones livin' yet that heard their forefathers sayin' they'd seen her, dressed in a wee yellow cloak that covered her from head to heels an' her runnin' out o' the corn into the next neighbour's field.'

There was a common belief, too, that the last man in a parish to have his corn cut did not get the Cailleach out of it that season unless he carried the last sheaf over three running burns or streams belonging to three different people!

The Cailleach sheaf was hung up inside the barn door and anybody going there to thresh was supposed to 'measure' the flail with his 'churn' as it was then called.

In Devon and Cornwall a similar custom was observed, the last sheaf being called the 'Neck', and in Northumberland this sheaf was dressed up and called the 'Kern Baby'.

In Scotland they had two uses for the last sheaf: one (when it was called the corn-maiden, Maighdean-Bhuana) in which the grains of corn in this precious sheaf were carefully preserved to mix with the seed of next season's sowing, and the other when the man who had first completed his harvesting made the sheaf into a rough resemblance of an old woman, then placed it in the field of a neighbour whose corn was still standing. This was called the Ghobhar Bhacach, lame goat, and its recipient had a lot of chaff to put up with until next harvest came along, when he went all out to beat the record for quick work!

The custom of gathering flowers on May Eve and hanging them up to keep evil spirits away is still common. The habit of lighting bonfires on St John's Eve, once general all over Ireland, is no longer observed in the Glens though it may still persist in other parts of the country.

Hallowe'en Customs

Some Hallowe'en customs, such as the burning of nuts and the running of lead through the wards of a key are by no means confined to the nine Glens, but other rites performed at this time do not seem to be generally known outside this area.

For instance, nowhere else have I heard of the kale-runt ceremony (a kale-runt, in case you do not know, is the stalk left standing in a field after the kale (cabbage) has been cut off it).

On Hallowe'en night, as it approaches the mystic time of midnight, girls with the marrying notion betake themselves to a field of kale, then, tightly closing their eyes (rather an unnecessary proceeding unless in strong moonlight) they enter the field and feel about for the stalks. Having at last grasped one they pull it out by the root, and rush back with it to the house. If, when examined, it is found to be below the average length of 'runts', then that girl's future partner will be a 'wee runt'!

A queer – and seldom practised – piece of magic was for the use of any girl in love with a lad who appeared indifferent to her charms. This girl had to get hold of a shirt belonging to the chosen victim (like Mrs Beeton's famous hare-soup recipe, this part was left to her own contriving!). She next had to wash it along with her own ('saving your presence') shift, and hang it to dry before the fire, and, if the spell worked, the owner of the shirt would feel an irresistible urge to visit the house wherein it hung.

The rest lay between his guardian angel and the girl!

Tale of a Shirt

Once upon a time there was a Glens girl who 'took a liking to' a young man living in the next townland. He was an only son and his mother, recently widowed, had been a girlhood friend of her mother who was also a widow with only one child.

Despite the fact that the girl had tried to intimate in various little ways that his addresses would not be unwelcome, the dense 'gulpin' didn't seem to notice this and treated her with a maddening friendliness.

At this juncture his mother came to visit the girl's house and discreet hints were received in a way that showed she would not be averse to having the girl as a daughter-in-law.

The time for plain speaking had come so the lovelorn lassie unburdened her mind. Ma was very sympathetic but at first could think of no sure way to overcome her son's indifference.

Suddenly she had an idea!

'Isn't next Tuesday Hall'eve?' she asked.

'It is,' replied the girl.

'Then I'll tell you what to do. When I'm washing Tom's shirts on Monday as usual, I'll send one over and you wash it with your —. It may be only an oul' 'freit', but it has worked before now.'

Blushingly Mary agreed and in due course the shirt was hung before the fire on Hallowe'en night, Mary staying up to see what happened.

Eleven o'clock came, half-past, a quarter to twelve; then just on the stroke of midnight her heart gave a bound as a knock came to the door.

'Come in,' she said faintly.

The latch lifted and in came – not the expected Tom but a dilapidated-looking old tramp!

'A'm kinda late,' said he, as he seated himself on the hob. 'A was for stayin' the night over in Mrs — 's (Tom's mother's) barn, but the young fella Tom an' me had words. He promised me a shirt he said was on the line and then when he couldn't get it he said A must hev stole it. Me! A niver took a ha-porth in my life didn't belong to me! Aye, a fine shirt it was, too, for A seen it on him many's a time.'

As he finished his indignant outburst his eyes strayed to the garment hanging on a chair in front of the fire and Mary noticed the start he gave.

'I suppose you'll be for our barn,' she said, to cover her trepidation.

Slowly he rose to his feet, then, looking her full in the face, he said:

'Naw! A'll be pushin' on to where there's more dacent people!'

Rooted to the spot, Mary watched him open the door, but ere he passed into the night he spoke again:

'Before the row, that Tom fella towl me to tell you he'd be over the morra night. His shirt shud be dry be then!'

And with this parting shot he disappeared.

The next evening Tom called at Mary's house as he had promised and she, by way of finally expressing her feelings, decided to confess that she had taken the shirt; she also told him about the old Hallowe'en custom which had motivated her.

Tom must have been more amenable to this forthright approach than to Mary's earlier hints for, although they had previously laughed at the old custom, Mary's action led in the end to the desired liaison. As for the tramp, even he fared not at all badly for whenever he happened to be in the neighbourhood again he was presented with a good deal more than a shirt!

A 'Blinking' Tale

There is another story current about a man who suspected that a neighbour of his had 'blinked' his cattle. Although he had ten cows of what had been a good milking strain and the neighbour had – through laziness and bad management – allowed his stock to fall to three sunken-backed 'rickles of bones', yet these three seemed to be giving more milk and better milk (if the quantity of butter the grocery carts got was a guide) than his.

Even Three-cow's few hens were giving better returns for their food while those of the ten-cow man went about as if ashamed of themselves, their heads down, and hardly laying an egg.

When this state of affairs had lasted for a couple of months the suspicion grew to almost certainty, so Ten-cow went off to visit a man well versed in such matters and told his tale of woe.

The old spell-breaker listened attentively, then suggested that he should visit Ten-cow's farm to see how and by whom the 'blinking' was being operated.

He duly arrived on night and next morning was taking a walk around the place when he spotted on the other side of the fence a man who had been banished from his native district years before for blinking the cattle of a widow who had refused to marry him.

The spell-breaker at once returned to the house and told Ten-cow, and suggested that as one of the beasts was due for calving that night they should both sit up with her.

At midnight they were seated in the byre, Spell-breaker with a shotgun across his knees, when they heard a fisslin' (rustling) at the door and next moment against the moonlight they saw silhouetted a great big hare!

It came slowly in, turning its head as if listening, then noticed the hurricane lamp whose dim light only made the shadowy corners more dark. It turned as if to flee, hesitated, then again approached the cow that was due to calve, touched her with its forepaws and then as she gave a loud 'Moo!' it wheeled and fled into the night.

During all this the two watchers, seated in a dark corner, had held their breath, lest they warn the intruder, but as it passed out of the door the man with the gun ran quickly into the moonlight 'caasey' or paved yard and fired a shot after it.

A scream like that of a hurt child came from the animal, but it went on, slowly enough for the pursuer to keep it in sight, and at last he saw a shadow passing inside the doorway of Three-cow's lighted kitchen. He cautiously followed, gun in hand, and as he entered the kitchen saw Three-cow helping to rip up the trouser-leg of another man. So fully occupied were they that he was beside them before they noticed him – and there was no use in subterfuge after that for on the stranger's leg from calf to thigh were the marks of the shot!

The spell-breaker never told what was said between the three of them but as soon as the 'quare fella' was able to walk he left that part of the country and Three-cow sold up and went to America.

Ten-cow was grateful to the spell-breaker and liberally rewarded him for ridding him of the shadow that had hung over his farm. His cows began again to fill the milk pails, and the cheerful cackling of hard-working hens sounded once more on the morning air.

The Banshee
Some superstitions die hard and belief in the existence of the banshee is one of them. The banshee is a little old woman usually only between two and three feet high and dressed in a dark cloak with the bonnet showing a white border round her face. She is never seen or heard until some tragedy is about to befall the family to which she is attached and none but a family of ancient ruling lineage can boast of (or should it be 'has to suffer') her visitations.

Such people as the O'Neills, O'Donnells, O'Kanes, McDonnells, McQuillans, McMullens or McAllisters among Ulster families are said to receive visits from one of the little ladies before a death occurs and in other parts of Ireland the O'Sullivans, O'Driscolls, O'Mahoneys and the O'Flahertys are similarly forewarned.

There is an old couplet :

By 'Mac' and 'O' you'll always know an Irishman they say,
But if they lack the 'O' or 'Mac' no Irishmen are they.

Some of the Norman-Irish families must have attained full status without having either, as the Fitzgerald, Fitzmaurice, Delargy and D'Arcy (or Darcy) names have traditions of banshee warnings.

Having been privileged to hear the banshee while she was lamenting the approaching death of an O'Neill, the writer can attempt to reproduce on paper the sound she made. Starting off with 'Och-O! Och-O!' she then went on, with increasing loudness until her voice reached a sort of shrieked: 'Och-O-Ee! Och-O-Ee! A-a-ah! O-O-O!' then it died down almost to a whisper and she intoned 'Aw-aw-aw!' then up with a dash to 'O-Ee! O-Ee! O-Ee!' and finishing on a sort of heartbroken cry that nothing but a long-sustained wailing note on a violin could illustrate.

Although three of us made a careful search around the house, and it was a fairly clear night, we could not see anything except a misty whiteness which two of us noticed hanging beside one of the chimneys. It moved about but the sound seemed to come from other parts of the building, front and back, and so we could not be certain if the patch of mist concealed the caoiner ('keener').

At one time, 'keening' at wakes and funerals was the general practice, the women relatives of the dear departed going through this performance at the bedside and graveside but it is unheard of nowadays.

Glens 'Wakes'

Wakes themselves were until twenty years ago the occasion of a lot of drinking and horseplay but today they are quiet reverential affairs visited almost exclusively by near friends and neighbours of the deceased person. In the old days when whiskey and tobacco were both plentiful and cheap, the male visitors were all given a jorum as soon as they arrived, together with a clay pipe.

Platefuls of coarse-cut plug tobacco were passed around,

from which the pipes were kept replenished and the bottle also made the rounds at intervals.

The womenfolk usually stayed in the 'room' with the corpse, their refreshment being cup after cup of tea, and their amusement – well, what do women talk about, anyway?

In the early hours of the morning, when most of the sitters-up began to get sleepy, all congregated in the kitchen and somebody usually started asking riddles.

It was at this stage in the proceedings that 'clodding' (throwing of pieces of peat and other forms of horseplay were indulged in, and in cases led to rows and recrimination, even to free-for-all fights).

The present custom is to keep open house on the first night after the death, the coffin being left in the church on the next night.

Funerals are usually attended by at least one member of every family in the district and, in the case of a person who was prominent in local affairs, by a representative of every house in the parish.

The New Year period has several taboos attached to it. On New Year's Eve the fire – banked up at night the year round – is allowed to die out, and is rekindled on New Year's Day. This superstition is supposed to be a survival of fire-worshipping times when on the 1st November was held the annual service, the sacred fire then lighted by the Druids being used to ignite torches which each householder carried home and placed on his hearthstone, carefully stoking and nursing the flame until the fire was well alight. Successful performance of this rite ensured a good fire all year but there was consternation if for any reason the torch became extinguished in transit.

Water is not to be thrown out on New Year's Day, neither is any money to be then, else for the rest of the year we are sure to be giving not receiving – and even if 'it is more blessed to give' yet …!

Red Hair Unlucky?

It is only to be expected that a part like the Nine Glens where so many men are or have been seafarers should have superstitions with a sea-tang. Killing sea-birds is considered unlucky, the otter or the seal are sacrosanct, and red-haired women are regarded as not nice to meet when going out for a day's fishing.

This antipathy to poor 'Carrots' has never been satisfactorily explained especially as it does not seem to apply to a red-haired man with the same force. There are many theories, one being that there was at one time a red-haired race here whose womenfolk intermarried occasionally with the black-haired people, such unions proving unhappy owing to the quick temper supposed to be characteristic of red-heads! A later-dated version declares that all copper-nobs, men and women, are unlucky since the day when Judas was guilty of betraying his Master.

St Brigid's Day, February 1, is marked by the preparation of crosses made of plaited rushes and suspended in every house, usually at the inside of a door. Earlier in our history there was a pagan goddess, Brigit, who was one of the most revered figures in Druidism.

Regarding the saint Brigid, she appears to have been confused with the pagan goddess or some other Brigid, as there is a tradition that there was a Brigid present in the stable at Bethlehem when Christ was born. As St Brigid was alive in the 6th century, she can hardly have been the same!

Taboos of the New-Born

The baptism of a child was attended by many taboos. The name chosen for the infant was not to be mentioned to the sponsors until the little one was ready to be taken to the church. The sponsors were to allow nobody else to carry the baby until after the ceremony and during the pouring of the water it was considered a good sign if it cried, some people going so far as to say that such crying was coming from the little devil driven out by the rite!

An unbaptised child who died was reckoned to have no right to burial in consecrated ground and the occasional burial-grounds we come across in remote spots are where such children are interred. Glenariff has one such spot, Crumnacur, where a low mound now overgrown with briars and hazels marks the site. (This place was used for another purpose some eighty-odd years ago, when the bodies washed ashore from a wreck were interred there in a common grave.)

In England the body of a suicide was at one time planted at a cross-roads, but the Nine Glens' custom in such cases was to bury the suicide just outside the confines of the graveyard, sometimes right against the wall surrounding it.

Don't cut a 'Skeog' Down!

There are many old-time superstitions still remembered, though now they are regarded only with amusement. 'Och, it's an oul' freit, but nobody believes in it nowadays' is a common enough saying. An exception is the superstition regarding 'fairy thorns' which is as cautiously respected as a century ago. The visitor may notice a bush growing right in the middle of somebody's ploughed field, and be mildly curious as to why it was not removed to allow the plough full scope.

Cut down a fairy thorn? Not likely!

Any Glensman would think twice before interfering with a fairy thorn – and then decide to leave it alone!

Numerous stories are told indicative of the dire consequences of such meddling with the wee people, from the one about the man who lost the eye to that of the maker of a mountain path who tried to save himself and his mates a lot of trouble by cutting down a fairy thorn right in the centre of the projected course. This rash mortal was found lying beside the almost unmarked base of the thorn tree, his hand clamped immovably around the saw and suffering severe pain in his right arm, pain that remained with him for almost a year afterwards.

Another case occurred as recently as 1920. This concerned a Glensman who took an axe to cut down a thorn that he thought was spoiling the look of one of his best fields.

His first stroke seemed to skid off the tough bark, and the point of the axe struck the toe cap of his boot which was luckily of stout leather and thus saved his toes from more than bruising.

Enraged by pain and the thought of his clumsiness, he swung a second and more determined blow at the thorn tree – and instantly a flow of what looked like blood started from the cut thus made in the bark!

The poor man was instantly brought to his senses when he saw this and, taking some leaves, he put them over the cut tree-trunk, binding them in place with a cord from his pocket.

He then made his way home to find his wife and son standing at the stable door. They beckoned him urgently and when he hobbled to them they pointed to one of the stands. There lay the better of his two horses, a gaping wound in its thigh.

Fairy thorns are called 'skeog' bushes and there are old people alive who declare that they have seen fairies dancing around them on a summer evening. Certain places, like Farusklin, in Glenariff, Scolgbuig in Galbolly, Tiveragh in Cushendall, or Feystown (above Glenarm) all have stories of fairies seen in their vicinity. Several little hills, some of them almost completely covered with thorn bushes, are avoided – as carefully as a townsman skirts a buried land-mine – by all wise people who say the bushes are 'gentle' bushes, the mounds the dwelling-place of fairies, and the eerie sounds that sometimes emanate from them are the fairy fiddles playing for a dance. Alice was never in such a Wonderland as these fairy palaces have seemed to the few people who have been allowed by the fairies to visit them. Time appears to slip past very quickly there and the visitor who has spent what he imagines to be a couple of days in one of these fairy domains is shocked when he returns to the ordinary world again, and finds that he has in fact been away a couple of years!

Three Weeks with the Fairies

There is an odd survival here and there of belief in 'changelings', and I have been pointed out an elderly woman who, it is said, spent three weeks with the fairies when a very young child. This idea arose in her case because she was missing for three weeks, then returned home at the end of that period showing no sign of distress but apparently without the slightest recollection of how she had spent the intervening time, nor has anyone been told that to this day! It certainly seems queer, even supposing that she had been kidnapped and then returned safe and well, that she retained not the faintest memory of those three weeks.

Witches and Wizards

Many of the people accused of witchcraft and wizardry really believed themselves to be in league with Old Nick, and their self-deception was so complete that they convinced their clients also. The weirdest concoctions, such as pulverised dried mice, frogs and human blood or even more loathsome ingredients, were solemnly presented, after much mumbo-jumbo, to a girl seeking a husband or a wife wanting a son, with instructions how they were to be used to produce the desired result.

At last, by their methods of 'raising the wind' in the monetary sense, their extortions turned public opinion so much against them that special Acts of Parliament were passed to deal with them, and official 'witch catchers' were appointed.

The most famous of these was a man called Hopkins, a native of Ipswich, who in the years 1644–47, was responsible for the deaths of hundreds of so-called witches, his fee per catch being £1. He had an absurdly simple – but infallible – test for anyone accused of witchcraft: tying the witch's right wrist to right ankle and left ditto, he and a helper cast her into a lake or river. If she floated, that was definite proof that she was supported by Satan, and if she sank that was just too bad for her, as she was innocent, but it was too late to do anything about it!

Nemesis overtook Hopkins after over three years of this. It may have been a 'frame-up' engineered by relatives of some of his victims, but when the charge of wizardry was brought against him his attempt at refutation by means of a pamphlet was successful and he was 'water-tested', found guilty, taken from the river and hanged.

Our Last Witchcraft Trial

It has been said that every man has his soft spot, some in the heart, some in the head. Where to place the average Glensman's belief in such things as witches or wizards is hard to know. He believes in them, even though he does not proclaim his belief too blatantly. Witches are not today subject to the punishment once meted out to them, when death or torture were considered as fitting their crime. The last case recorded in Ireland of a trial for witchcraft was that at Carrickfergus in 1711, when eight elderly women were arraigned on a charge of having used their 'black art' on Mary Dunbar, of Islandmagee, a girl of 18.

It was customary for pilloried malefactors to be pelted with mud and the like by the jeering crowd that usually congregated to enjoy the spectacle, but in this case worse missiles were used for one woman – in the words of a contemporary writer – 'had an eye beated out'.

The pillory was a wooden instrument of punishment in use until 1837, and consisted of two movable boards through which the victim's head and hands were put, the contraption being commonly erected on a scaffold. The offences for which it was the usual punishment were forgery, perjury or libel, but from 1815 until its abolition the only crime punished by the pillory was perjury. That 'witchcraft' was regarded as perjury is another proof that 'the law's a Hass', for many of the 'witnesses' in such a case must have given false 'evidence' on oath.

Witchcraft and wizardry have been mentioned from the earliest times and only a very few of these early scribes ventured to record unbelief – not even Shakespeare, who seems to have kept an open mind on the subject. In Reginald Scott's *Discoverie of Witchcraft*, however, is the following unorthodox pronouncement:

'No one endued with common sense but will deny that
the elements are obedient to witches and at their
commandment, or that they may at their pleasure send
hail, rain, tempest, thunder and lightning, when she
being but an old woman casteth a flint stone over her left
shoulder toward the west, or hurleth a little sea-sand up
into the element, or wetteth a broom sprig in water and
sprinkleth the same into the air, or diggeth a pit into the
earth and, putting water therein, stirreth it about with
her fingers, or boileth hog's bristles, or layeth sticks
across upon a bank where never a drop of water is, or
buryeth sage until it be rotten; all which things are
confessed by witches, and affirmed by writers to be the
means that witches use to raise extraordinary tempests
and rain.'

James VI of Scotland (who later became James I of England)
was an authority on the subject and seems to have believed in the
power of witches to conjure up storms at will. In his *Demonology*
he quotes, as proof of this, his own experience when bringing his
bride from Denmark. A terrible storm arose, blowing directly
against the Royal Ship, though other vessels accompanying them
had a fair wind!

They managed at last to make the passage to Leith, where
inquiries set on foot by James revealed that a certain Dr Fian and
Agnes Simpson were both believed to be practising sorcery.

The suspects were arrested, tortured and at last 'confessed',
giving full particulars of the means they used in raising the wind!

In one of the ancient tales referring to the landing of the
different races in Ireland, we read that the Druids of the Firbolgs

conjured up a tempest to scatter the fleet of the invading Milesians, so this wind-raising business goes back a long way, and there is the story already related of the Campbelltown horse to show that it has continued to fairly recent times.

8

A Night by a Glens Fireside

It should be noted that the name 'Glens of Antrim', as commonly applied to the waterfalls of Glenariff, is a misnomer. There are nine principal glens on Antrim's seaboard, and a person might as well say he had visited 'The Towns of County Antrim' after a day in Ballymoney as claim to have seen 'The Glens' after a look at Ess-na-Larach waterfall!

During our tour of the Nine Glens you have never been inside a house except the Torr Head watch-house and the kitchen where we saw the butter being made. That could hardly happen on any Glens tour for the people are as hospitable as can be found anywhere and we are more likely to be embarrassed by the number of invitations we receive.

Let us call at Charlie — 's house, a typical farmhouse set at the foot of a steep hill where a few friends have gathered to 'ceilidh' this winter night.

From our first knock at the door, followed by an instant, 'Come in!' we are made to feel at home. There is no formality about our welcome. A chair, a seat on the settlebed, or even the ingle-nook ('hob') are offered to us and the conversation is resumed where it was interrupted by our entrance. Somebody asks us a question or addresses a remark to us and soon we are taking our full share in the 'crack'.

Meanwhile, the woman o' the house, or one of the daughters, has been making trips to and from 'the room' and within a short time of our arrival we are invited to 'Come on down and have a mouthful o' tay. You'll be hungry after your walk.'

The conventional reply to this as you rise to follow your hostess is, 'Och, this is a lot o' trouble I'm giving you,' which is invariably answered, 'Trouble? No trouble at all makin' a drop o' tay. I'm sorry we haven't anything very fancy.'

Thus prepared for austerity, you enter the room to find a table sagging with a most appetising spread of good country produce. Soda farls cut in convenient hunks, piled up 'fadge' (potato-bread), some home-made oven-pot cake and a brace of lovely big brown eggs catch your eye, then a couple of 'prints' of golden butter and (as you are a visitor) a cut baker's loaf and a plate of bought biscuits. Home-made jams, real cream in the jugs, and tea that beats – aye, and often in price, too! – the best any first-class hotel in London could offer, are there for your delectation, and unless you do full justice to the fare your hosts are likely to be displeased and to think that you didn't find it good enough for you.

We are soon doing our best to transfer the sag from the table to ourselves and some time later we return to the kitchen, feeling full, among other things, of benevolence towards the world in general!

The chat becomes more lively, then somebody suggests a song from Dan — . This idea seems popular, so Dan clears his throat and in a pleasing tenor sings an old ballad called *The Maid of Lurgan Green*. Hearty applause follows then a pretty little grey-eyed girl is coaxed for 'her pleasure' which turns out to be a charming wee song about two lovers who meet unexpectedly after being estranged for some time: 'He looked, she looked, they looked away, but somehow then a tear – she knew not how it came about – did on her cheek appear. He'd taken but another glance, that tear he chanced to spy, with opened arms he beckoned her, she into them did fly' – and, of course, orange blossoms and roses all the way, let us hope!

It doesn't take more than half an eye to see that there is one young man present who is deeply interested in this song – or might it be the singer? At any rate, as Nancy sits down again his glance speaks some message she seems to understand, judging by her blush!

A short silence falls, broken by the man o' the house, who reaches up to a shelf behind him for his fiddle-case, and says, 'We'll have a dance to warm yez up. What'll it be, a 'set' or a reel?'

'A set!' is the eager answer.

'All right, grab your partners; ye boys ye!' And soon he is making the bow fly in a rollicking tune, while each lad takes a lassie and leads her to a place on the floor.

You are maybe a little diffident at first but something tells you that the aloof-looking beauty over there with the glorious red curling hair has thrown you an encouraging glance so you approach her and find that she accepts with a fleeting smile that makes even your base heart quicken a trifle.

The dance over, you are glad to sit down to recover your wind, though their hard and healthy life has made these young people able to dance for hours without exhaustion.

Other songs and dances follow, then by general consent the ring is formed round the fireplace again, and we all take part in animated discussion of passing events – mostly local – or of story-telling. Tales of fairy or of freit, of banshee or of ghost, some traditional and some (from the older folk) reminiscent, are told in that kitchen with its fragrant turf fire (until fairly recently most of such fires were 'on the hearth', i.e. at floor level), its 'crane' and 'crook' supporting a three-legged pot full of stirabout (oaten porridge). The firelight is reflected back from the gleaming dishes on the dresser, outside a bleak winter wind may be blowing but within all is warmth and friendliness.

Homeward Bound

At last the time comes to take our leave and we bid our host and his family farewell, the other ceilidhers leaving with us. At the foot of the loaning we part from them also, with mutual expression of the hope that we may spend another such night together again some time.

They go their way, we ours, while in the house we have left the members of the family join in prayer and then betake themselves to bed, leaving the kitchen to a silence broken only by the cheerful chirping of the crickets on the hearth, near the banked-up fire.

We have come now to within sight of the end of the road and those readers who have accompanied me from the beginning of our tour may or may not agree with the sentiment expressed in Sam Weller's reply to his respected parent:

'That's rayther a sudden pull up, ain't it, Sammy?' inquired Mr Weller.

'Not a bit on it,' said Sam, 'she'll vish there wos more, and that's the great art o' letter writin'.'

Well, I have enjoyed writing it and I hope you have enjoyed reading it sufficiently well to wish there was more.

We have visited most of the places of interest in the Nine Glens, we have heard the history of most of its more famous inhabitants, past and present, and listened to stories from its folklore; we have seen its people at work and at play, at sea and on the land; we have allowed some of its characters to strut once again upon the stage; we have been introduced to Glens poets, from 'Dusty Roads' (James Studdert Moore), James Gorman or 'Poet' Alexander McKie to 'Cut Rock' James Kelly, so by now we should feel like natives of the place and feel also that a visit there is a sort of homecoming.

If I have aroused in your mind a desire to see for yourself this seacoast corner of Antrim, my success is complete, for anyone who has visited Antrim's lovely Nine Glens has always fallen under their spell. It is not only the exiled Glensman who has felt a tug at his heart-strings upon hearing such names as Glenarm, Glencloy, Glenariff, Glen Ballyeamon, Glenaan, Glencorp, Glendun, Glentaisi or Glenshesk, but also the soldiers of many nations who passed some time amongst us.

Here we are at the end of the road, so we must say 'goodbye' and as most of the chapters in our Tour contained a 'varse' or two we'll have to compose something to round off the journey.

Around the Nine Glens

Glenarm and Carnlough
From green Glenarm to Rathlin Isle,
And glens that lie between,
Our course has followed Antrim's coast
Through many a change of scene.
We've watched the 'Sliding Village',

And talked of good 'Queen Anne',
We've heard the Doonan waterfalls
Make music as they ran.

Galbolly
We've followed Jasper Fairey
Till to Galbolly he went,
And wondered what befell him then,
And who his savings spent.
We've seen that hidden hamlet
Bereft nine months of sun,
Then sailed across Red Bay to look
Where lived Lord Cushendun

Glenariff
Glenariff, Queen of all the Nine
From Parkmore to the shore,
We've seen its Ess-na-Larach Fall
And church at old Kilmore;
Cairn-Neill, and Lurigedan's crest,
Where chieftain Finn McCool
Once exercised Fianna
At his military school.

Garron Tower
We've coasted round the Garron Head,
And seen the building grand
Erected by the Marchioness when
Famine stalked the land.
We've spent an hour at Garron Tower,

Roaming its gardens fine,
And thought how many lives she saved
Throughout that awful time.

A Dog's Grave

We've seen the grave where Urisk lies
And read his epitaph,
At first amused, and then confused,
Then lost desire to laugh,
This tribute to a faithful friend
Exhorts us, if we can,
To bear in mind dogs we can find
More loyal far than man.

A Chieftain's Grave

We've seen the stone encasing bones
Of prehistoric chief;
Our digging broke an urn that spoke
Of some old-time belief
That life is but a interlude,
Valhalla lies beyond,
Where dead exist, unhemmed by cist,
Or other human bond.

Cushendall

We've made a call on Cushendall
 A village 'neat' and clean,
Where Curfew tower doth seem to glower
At visitors I ween.
In Ballyeamon we have strayed to pick its flora rare,
Or crossed to Poet Ossian's Grave
On Lubitavish there.

The Battle of Aura

On Aura, where McQuillan's clan
McDonnells trapped and slew,
We journeyed o'er the pitted ground
And fought the fight anew.
We visited McQuillan's grave,
And Hugh McFeelim's stone,
Then pictured how the armies lay
In Fifteen-ninety-one.

The 'Brae' Road

From Cushendun we though it fun
To walk across to Torr,
Till on that path we found with wrath
A surface to abhor.
The way was rough, the going tough,
Came, ere we ceased to hike,
Pat Hamilton on Torr-ward run
With pillion motor-bike!

'The Big Shower'

In 'ninety-five there's men alive
In Cushendun who tell
How in that year, they felt with fear
The shower of hail that fell –
'The month was June, yet very soon
Culraney's top was white
And overhead we saw with dread
A sky as black as night.'

Hail like Pigeon's Eggs!

'The thunder pealed, and as we kneeled
In terror 'neath a bank
The sun appeared, the darkness cleared
Though air with brimstone stank.
As – fearful still – we left the hill,
'Twas strange to wee bare feet,
When, stepping through that icy 'broo'
Below they felt the heat.

The Rescue

We've heard how yacht in trouble got
With honeymooners two;
And S.O.S. in their distress
Brought coastguard rescue crew
From Torr nearby, whose gallant try
To reach the man and wife
With breeches buoy, much to their joy
Succeeded, saved their life.

Fairies and Sea-Tales

We've read of 'charm' to save from harm,
Of leprechaun and wraith,
Or had to dree the weird banshee
Come heralding a death.
From Robertson or Dorey's men,
And Kelly's too, as well,
We've heard the tale of war or gale
And Dunkirk beach's hell.

Ballycastle

Our thoughts have run to where the nun
Of Bun-na-Margy fame
Forgot the 'greatest virtue' when
She saw her sister's shame.
We've traced in Ballycastle town
Where Boyd's ambitious schemes
To make it Antrim's foremost port
Turned out to be but dreams.

'Nuts and Yella-man'

Throughout the trip we've tried to skip
The doleful or the dull,
And from our folklore treasure-house
The brightest tried to cull.
We've eaten 'dulse and yella-man'
In Ballycastle found,
And laughed to see the jolly spree
When Lammas Fair came round.

Glens Ceilidh – Farewell

We spent a night in Charlie's house
In song, and dance, and crack,
And at the close old Charlie said
He hoped we'd soon come back.
Well, that may be, some day (D.V.),
When, granted time and tide,
We'll meet again, so, until then,
Good Wishes –

Jack McBride